I0791382

Other books by the same author, to include pen names

Fiction

Antipodes 10, by John Pascal
Antipodes 20, by John Pascal
The Imposture & Other Tales; Thirty Short Stories, by John Pascal
The Shaggy Dog and Other Stories, by John Pascal
The Dartist, by John Pascal
Travels With My Ass, by John Pascal
The Resurrection of Charles Witchway, by John Pascal

Non-Fiction

Polwar: The Politicization of Armed Forces, by Pascal R. Politano
A Sharp Seasoning of Truth: A Comprehensive Commentary in the Pursuit of Genuine National Security, by Pascal R. Politano
Refractions, by Pascal R. Politano
Solo: A Guide for Men Whose Fate is Not to Endure the Raptures of Marriage, by Atticus Grammaticus
The Modern Day Gentleman and Other Essays, by Atticus Grammaticus

Poetry

The Man in the Moon, by Pascal R. Politano
Painting the Lily, by Pascal R. Politano
A Poet's Choice, by Pascal R. Politano

AS DARKNESS FALLS
FROM NOTES TAKEN DURING THE GREAT PANDEMIC
2020-2021

PASCAL R. POLITANO

authorHOUSE

vincit veritas

AuthorHouse™
1663 Liberty Drive
Bloomington, IN 47403
www.authorhouse.com
Phone: 833-262-8899

Published by AuthorHouse 09/15/2021

ISBN: 978-1-6655-3365-2 (sc)
ISBN: 978-1-6655-3364-5 (e)

Library of Congress Control Number: 2021915576

Print information available on the last page.

Any people depicted in stock imagery provided by Getty Images are models, and such images are being used for illustrative purposes only.
Certain stock imagery © Getty Images.

This book is printed on acid-free paper.

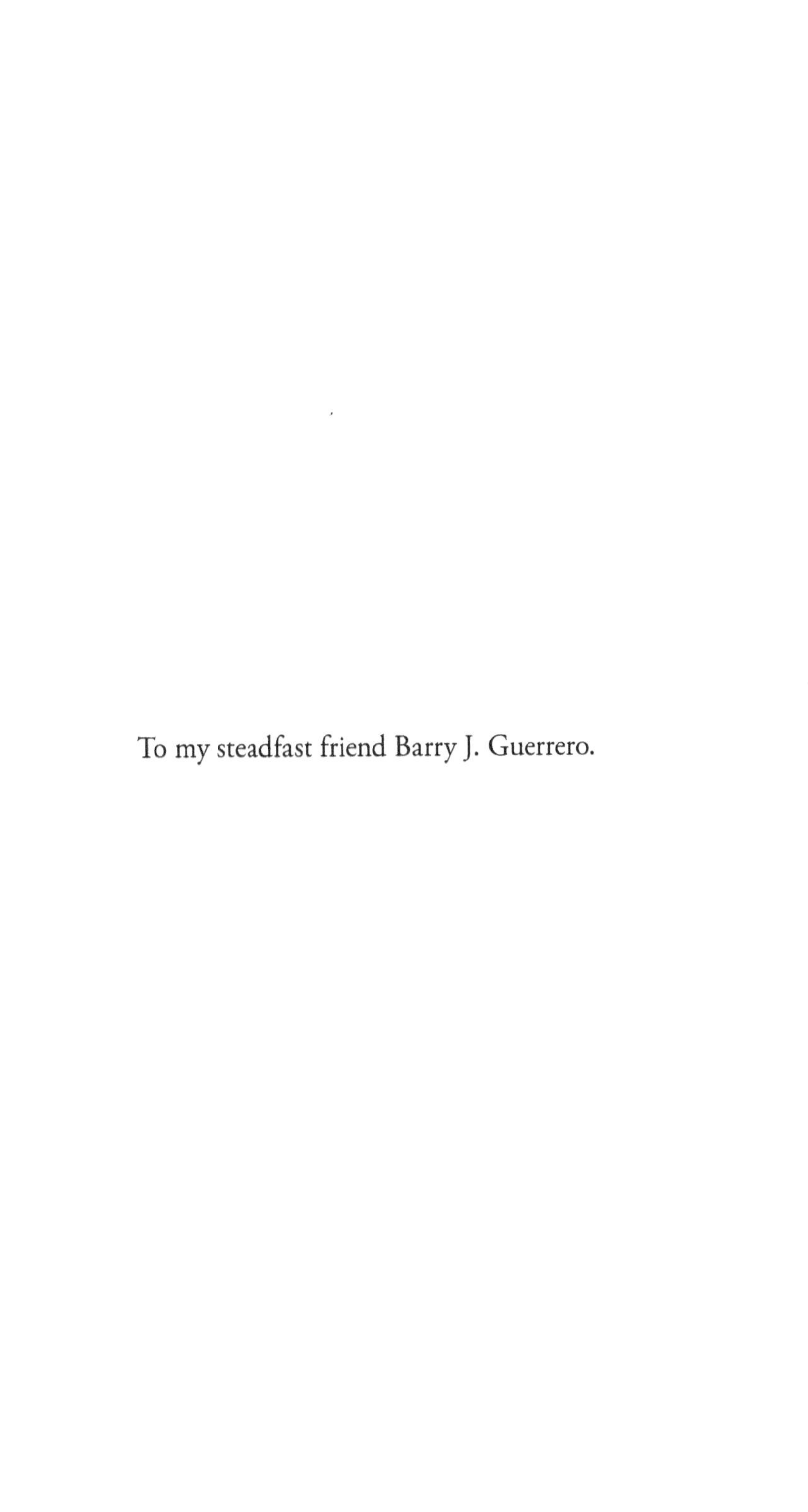

To my steadfast friend Barry J. Guerrero.

ACKNOWLEDGEMENT

This small but comprehensive exposition was in great part made possible with the able and cheerful assistance of Suzanne Politano and Gail Kiser.

AUTHOR'S NOTE

This small book has been compiled from open letters written from March 2020 to July 2021 during the heart of The Great Pandemic, which continues with such tenacity at a time when we are faced with other grave crises of a more mundane nature. The author hopes that the criticisms, suggestions, and concepts contained herein may be helpful to all Americans in these perilous and threatening times.

April 1, 2020

It was bound to come. Medical scientists during the Obama administration gave dire warnings that we were due for a great pandemic; these were passed on to Trump's transition team in 2018 and were promptly ignored by Trump and his staff. Now, the scourge comes as a double danger. Added to the fact of its ease of transmission and its mortality rate, it detracts from and deflects attention from the even greater catastrophe which looms inexorably and will mark the end of life as we know it for the entire planet—that which will result from climate change—specifically, global warming. Our thoughts may be diverted to some extent when those forest fires, inevitable now, begin in California and elsewhere in the West. And what a time this would be for some "enemy," real or abstract ("terrorism"), to bring down our entire power grid! If India should detonate a nuclear weapon over Islamabad, what would we do? What *could* we do? The only conceivable event that would preempt this great plague would be an invasion by alien creatures from deep space.

Almost seven hundred years ago, a ship from the Levant docked at a southern European port. A rat carrying fleas infected with bubonic plague arrived aboard that ship.

Within two years, one third to over half the population of Europe was dead.[*]

President Trump probably would have labeled that tragedy the "Arab" or "Muslim" plague rather than the Black Death, as we have come to know it. And he would agree readily to calling that more recent pandemic of 100 years ago which killed fifty million people, the "Spanish" Influenza,[†] much as with his xenophobic prejudice, he now claims that: "We are under attack by a 'Chinese' virus." Ironically, China has fought the recent plague heroically and as of this writing, has stabilized it and is winning its battle.

If the United States were given the responsibility of quelling the virus globally, the mortality rate would be no less than the "Spanish" or "Arabic" pandemics of the past, despite all the medico-scientific advances we have made. Not for the first time our "defensive" achievements have gone from SNAFU to TARFU, to FUBAR[‡] with lightning speed under President Trump's insane "management." Under the Federal Production (or Procurement) Act invoked by President Truman in 1950 during the Korean War, Trump could, simply by an executive order, *mandate* that any corporate entity in the US must retool-reorganize their production capabilities to provide the wherewithal for combatting the virus. As just two examples: Hanes could start making masks, gowns, etc.; and the electronics sector, ventilators. Further, an OPA (Office

---

[*] See Barbara Tuchman's *A Distant Mirror: The Calamitous 14th Century,* 1978.

[†] The "Spanish" flu had its origin in the trenches of the Western Front among the Allied (French-English) forces in the Great War.

[‡] Situation normal; all fouled up; things are really fouled up; fouled up beyond all recognition. GI situation commentaries used during WWII. "Fouled" obviously has been substituted for another old Anglo Saxon word.

of Price Administration) reinstated to suppress price gouging as did FDR's administration during WWII. At the same time, rationing should also be reinstated to avoid hoarding.

Catastrophic also will be the economic impact of the Corona Virus. If I survive this latest scourge, I'll derive some consolation from that impact. I've mentioned (too many times) to family and friends how when I was young, and for a number of years beyond the Great Depression and the War as well, "Everything cost a nickel – from a candy bar to a phone call to a ride, anywhere, on the subway."* Those who survive the virus may well experience that as a reality. And should the government refuse to bail out those Wall Street moguls as they did so shamelessly in 2008-09 instead of fining them in billions and sending them to prison, I'm looking forward to watching them jumping to their deaths from tall buildings on live TV.

Meanwhile, TV commercials continue to tout such frivolous things as cosmetics. And the *CNN news* room comes on with "…glad to have you with us." Soon they may have to amend this to say "…glad you are *still* with us." In addition, Dr. Sanjay Gupta of CNN is earning his star on the Hollywood's Walk of Fame.

As to Trump's possible reelection, I await one of his advisors to recall FDR's slogan during his 1944 campaign for a fourth term at the height of WWII; "don't change horses in the middle of the stream!" In any case, if he survives the virus, Andrew Cuomo probably will run for president in 2024 and quite possibly will win the election.

---

* And let's not forget those "loosie" cigarettes for a penny a piece which were sold at the shop door.

Finally, as for me, if I don't survive this satanic bug, I'll just: "Tell St. Peter at the Pearly Gate that I hates to make him wait, but I just gotta have another cigarette!"

Addendum: When I was in grammar school and the world's population stood at about two billion people, that of the U.S. was less than one half what it is now. I never felt crowded unless I was in downtown New York. Perhaps it's time for an adjustment…except for the tragic consequences it will produce for the "have-nots" of our populace. Meanwhile, I'm pleased to see Trump's beloved stock exchange down among the wines and spirits.

In the previous letter on the pandemic I suggested re-invoking such agencies and measures as an office of price fixing, and I might have added that encouraging the public to plant victory gardens (as during the second World War) should be considered. To my amusement I now see and hear public service announcements suggesting that very thing. Perhaps because of the astronomical bailout required to try to stabilize the already failing national economy the Government might begin offering defense or war bonds, similar but with price adjustments suitable to compensate for inflation, to those issued during the same era. Certainly, in view of the massive financial blood-letting, the latter resort is not inconceivable.

But enough of these fruitless, whimsical speculations. The country is becoming a shambles, and if we survive the ravages of the COVID-19 virus we'll be faced with the less silent but equally tangible devastation of an economic collapse which we as a people may no longer have the strength of character, collectively, needed to restore our society to some state of stability. We were able to do it in the 1930s and '40s during a deep depression followed by a global war. I fervently hope that we have not become too soft, too weak, too self-indulgent, and too morally corrupt to do it.

As early as 13 February 2017 a group of thirty-five psychiatrists, psychologists, and social workers published a letter in *The New York Times* which said, in part: "Mr. Trump's speech and actions make him incapable of serving as president…a form of narcissism that affects a person's ability to perform." Trump, driven by this narcissistic disorder, continues to tempt fate now with his reckless insistence upon "reopening the country with a bang" for purely financial reasons at the behest of his Wall Street cronies. What he has done and continues to do in his stubborn and wrongheaded mismanagement of the COVID-19 crisis constitutes nothing less than a major felony; to wit, the facilitation of mass homicide, in this case what might even be called genocide, for his own selfish purposes and self-aggrandizement. If that isn't grounds for his removal from office what is? He and his trumpery miscreants in the White House should be brought to justice under the provisions of the Twenty-Fifth Amendment to the Constitution. Clearly, Trump has demonstrated that he is unable to discharge the powers and duties of his office. Must he institute a program of mass imprisonment, or worse, against those who do not support him or, in his paranoia, are plotting against him before the public comes to its senses and takes some action? Ironically, in our semi-helplessness in defending ourselves from this modern plague — mitigation by "distancing" is our main defense thus far — we have lost our right of public assembly under the Constitution. Those mass protests against the Vietnam War played no insignificant part in ending that misbegotten and mismanaged fiasco. Mad as he may be, the President, with his undeniable cunning, almost undoubtedly is aware of this limitation and is taking full advantage of it.

In these dire circumstances, if removing him under the 25th Amendment failed, truly poetic justice would be served if Trump contracted the disease and died of it. Barring that and in the extreme, the only way of ridding ourselves of this excrescence — one of Nature's worst blunders — would be by assassination. And it seems to me that in such a case the ends of true justice would also be well-served if the perpetrator(s) were apprehended and tried, the jury would bring in a verdict of not guilty on the grounds of justifiable homicide.

The virus doesn't know or respect boundaries or borders anymore than those stately trees I spoke of elsewhere when writing about another of those awesome apocalyptic Horsemen.[*] That was war in its traditional, clamorous sense; now we are confronted by a silent but still deadly enemy. Trump's harsh and gratuitous announcement that he, as "Commander-in-Chief" in this "war" had the sole authority to "reopen the country" was utter nonsense. Constitutionally, under the Tenth Amendment, "The powers not delegated to the United States by the Constitution, nor prohibited by it to the States, are reserved to the States respectively, or to the people." I doubt that Trump has a personal copy of the Constitution; if he has he's probably never read it; he's certainly never studied it. In addition to that Tenth Amendment he undoubtedly knows nothing of other lawful barriers to the achievement of his imperious threats, such as dual federalism, divided sovereignty, or the right

---

[*] q.v. "The Snowman" in *A Poet's Choice*, © 2019 by Pascal R. Politano.

of association. If we, the people, don't do *something* about this madman — who makes Mad King George III, against whose sovereignty we rebelled two and one-half centuries ago, look like the soul of sanity, rectitude and serenity — if we merely acquiesce to his narcissistic whims, we will be signing our own death warrants.

Justice without power is helpless; power without justice is tyranny.

W hat to do? Thousands of gallons of milk being poured down the drains; farmers plowing-under acres of fresh vegetables they didn't bother to harvest; thousands of pigs and chickens being "euthanized" and relegated to the refuse pits. Meanwhile, mile-long lines of vehicles inching ahead with their occupants waiting hours to reach the distribution points of food pantries, while hoping the supply won't run out before they get there…. What to do? A leader worthy of the title, invoking the Federal Production Act of 1950, would order the establishment of a food redistribution office or agency with a tough-minded, top-flight businessman to administer it (not an inept civil servant). This person would have absolute authority to order motor transport, rail and air freight companies to do his bidding. Under his authority those food supplies now being wasted would be identified, while locations throughout the country with the greatest need are selected. Then, under strict supervision by law enforcement agencies at all levels, to avoid hoarding, black marketeering, and other malpractices, distribution would be efficiently carried out. Volunteers with experience in food handling-distribution would be harnessed and paid a fair wage to staff and operate the distribution centers (many would volunteer their services). A true leader would do this. The entire matter of proper leadership would insist upon it, as well as other measures, in as grave a time as this.

During WWII, with competent and good advisors, not bungling sycophants, FDR was able to see us successfully through *that* war. Today, we hear government officials and news outlets telling us that once again we are at war. Perhaps, instead of just stopping there with that allusion, the executive branch of government should carry the analogy further, so that they are clear on what they can do about it besides merely alluding to the fact. In a previous open letter I gave as examples agencies and instruments which are made possible under the conditions of war by the War Production Board and its sweeping authority. Just as the States' militias are mobilized, other entities in the civilian sector become subject to federal authority at such times.

The *Dictionary of American Politics* defines the War Production Board as: A federal wartime agency created by executive order, January 16, 1942 to control production and procurement of supplies for military purposes. It was abolished in 1945, after the war ended, and superseded by Truman's Federal Production Act in 1950. Less known is the war profits tax, the burden of which is intended to fall directly upon profits of private enterprise attributable to war contracts or to abnormal wartime demand for goods and services. Witness the competition and consequent price gouging that the States are faced with today in their desperate attempts to procure the items needed to battle the virus. War powers are constitutionally committed to the executive and legislative branches of government to wage war, raise, organize, equip, and command the necessary public forces, and to apply such regulations affecting personal liberty (social distancing, quarantine, use of face masks, closing of schools, theaters, shops, etc.), and the national economy as the exigencies of war may require. When fully applied as a result of an emergency, war powers are broader in scope than any other powers of government, especially of the general governance in a federal system such as that of the United States. If we're in a war and must fight it, for God's sake let's get on with it!

President Trump calls governors and asks what they need to fight this war. What they need is leadership. In a situation such as this the states cannot be expected to "see it through" on their own and individually. No matter how heroically they may strive to defeat the enemy virus, each in its own way, they cannot do it as disparate entities without centralized, cohesive leadership. As General Patton said, "You can't lead from the rear. It's like trying to move a strand of wet spaghetti by getting behind it and pushing." One finger may have its uses, but closing all five produces a fist.

Now, thanks to this classic example of disorganization, we have the dubious distinction of having a third of all virus cases in the world and a quarter of its deaths. A fundamental reason for this lies in testing and contact tracing for the virus, or, more precisely, our lack of them. While Trump boasts that we lead the rest of the afflicted countries in testing, the truth is that we lag woefully behind due almost entirely to the government's ineptitude, Trump's arrogance, and his fear that the number of those infected would rise exponentially. Incidentally, we have achieved our dubious distinction while comprising less than one fifth of the world's population.

As a separate issue, much as I don't like hitting a man when he's already down, one great problem cannot mask another. As that fewer than five percent of the global population applies to the number of virus cases we've tallied, so too does it apply to drug addiction. Sixty-five percent of all illicit drugs are consumed in America.

Finally, I suggest that those fly-by tributes to our "frontline soldiers" be replaced by hazardous duty pay.

In another open letter I'll discuss the economic breakdown coincidental with the pandemic.

Truly, we find ourselves on the horns of a great dilemma: viz., science versus the economy. On one side we must face a dreadful pandemic from which we have little defense, no protective vaccine, nor even an efficacious therapeutic treatment. Our only resort thus far is mitigation: distancing socially, wearing masks, isolation or quarantine, testing, and contact tracing. Therein lies the rub. Against our urge toward self-preservation is arrayed the tangible need to go on with our "normal" lives in order to preserve and satisfy our material and social needs as a society of human beings.

A typical manifestation of this terrible dilemma is the closing of schools as one means of mitigating the spread of the disease. With young children staying home for an indeterminate period of time how can parents also stay home when they must work to earn a livelihood? (if indeed they still have a job to go to). Now, to alleviate this problem somewhat, a system, however haphazard, of "virtual schooling" has been resorted to so that children can continue with their educations at home using the internet.*

---

* Given their present obsessions with TV and video games and now virtual schooling at home, perhaps future generations will be born with square eyes.

However, since eighteen million homes throughout the U.S. lack high-speed internet service this leaves a considerable gap in satisfying the problem. Here I could suggest a possible solution. Someone such as Mark Zuckerberg of Facebook fame (or at least notoriety) could be put in charge of a federal home schooling system. The Government, through him, could then provide those eighteen million families with the equipment they need and someone to teach them how to use it. To complicate this problem further, is the inequitable (and iniquitous) distribution of wealth in this country, which makes it common for both parents to work outside the home. Somewhat related to this procedure, I could suggest that temporarily suspended (due to social distancing) college students be recruited to help in the accomplishment of contact tracing, for which thousands of people will be needed. Similarly, medical students in the same situation could be rallied to be trained and deployed to perform the multitudinous tests that are so desperately needed, in a timely fashion.

Scandalous also is the fact that, abetted by the federal government, relief money in the trillions has been diverted by the banks whose duty was to distribute it fairly, to their favorite clients: high-profile companies and corporations such as the airlines and their suppliers—Boeing, oil companies, and the like. Small and medium-sized farmers, once the backbones of this nation, are faring no better. The lion's share of the latest twenty-eight billion-dollar relief fund approved by Congress has been diverted to the huge agribusiness corporations, and this comes on the heels of President Trump's tariff war with China, not least to those soy bean growers who depended on China's insatiable appetite for the commodity.

Then, of course, there is the all-too-human tendency among Americans to socialize, and this includes dining out, jollifications at clubs and bars, attending concerts and theaters, and not least, sports events. Of more importance is peoples' need to shop for food and other household items, and personal necessities, real or perceived, such as haircuts, salon visits, and not least, medical services not necessarily connected with the virus.

The jobless rate in the U.S. has now equaled, some say exceeded, that of the Great Depression: some 20-25 percent. Barring a small miracle (such as the early discovery of a safe and effective vaccine), people will begin to starve, literally, and with more firearms than there are people in the U.S. we may see violence on a dramatic scale, far exceeding those bread riots in France that preceded their revolution in 1789. Jean Valjean merely stole a loaf of bread to feed his children. We may see armed marauders everywhere looting what shops may still be open, and then even private homes will no longer provide safe refuge. While trying to endure the extant catastrophe, the U.S. will be subjected to a perverted, simplistic and malignant form of social Darwinism; a barbaric period of survival of the fittest. We're in for a long ride on this ghost train, whatever its destination may turn out to be.

A final note on the health side of all our problems lies in a situation which the federal government has done its best to suppress. Within the general populace there are millions of people who, if they haven't lost their jobs yet, earn just enough so that they don't qualify for Medicaid, but who cannot afford medical health insurance. A sad commentary on what our boastful liar of a president is pleased to call the greatest nation in the history of the world.

During the Second World War the Russians suffered the destruction of 700 of their towns and villages, and millions of her people, both military and civilian, were killed. Our Civil War, terrible as it was, becomes a microcosm compared to this sort of devastation. Ultimately, as the Germans were being blasted to bits under the auspices of Churchill and Air Marshal "Bomber" Harris, with the able assistance of our Eighth Air Force, the Russians, exhausted but triumphant, began to put their country back together. Having buried their dead, they began to rebuild those towns and villages. They also reestablished and strengthened their system of governance. In short, they never gave up. They survived that horrific experience and emerged as one people, (without the partisan politics we must endure in this time of crisis), stronger than they were before it. Unfortunately, under their system of governance their doctrines and ideologies were inimical, in fact, diametrically opposed, to those held by most Americans; unfortunate also was the fact that mainly because of their decisive victory over the Germans they emerged as a superpower, and it was those two factors that gave rise to the Cold War*. But the politics of all this is not the object lesson here. The object lesson is one of survival. The Germans, after the war, rebuilt, actually restored, all those ancient and stately buildings destroyed by the Allied bombings, and did it within just a few years. Do we, as a people, as a nation, have the moral fiber and discipline, and

---

* And if we're not careful we'll be entering another cold war, this time with China.

not least the patience, to survive, and prosper, in this, the greatest disaster, the greatest trial in *our* history?

Whatever happens if we survive this modern-day plague, I hope it puts "paid" to this absurd political correctness run amok and to all the meaningless hugging.

I t won't take a crystal ball to see what the future holds. With world-wide "reopening" after social distancing, self-isolation and quarantines, the spread of the Corona virus will increase significantly. But aside from the death toll coincident with people desperate to survive economically, the balance of any equity in our have-have not society is tipping dangerously close to a state of pandemonium, literally, a battle for survival.

A first effect in the economic turmoil is seen in the rise in retail prices. The "haves" are desperate to maintain their financial position, and are compensating for lack of control over the production and distribution of food and other necessities by raising prices, in some cases outrageously. This will continue until the vast majority of people just can't afford to pay these prices (recent reliable sources tell us that forty-two percent of businesses and consequently, jobs, will never recover from their shutdowns). Then prices will begin to fall, precipitously, and, though there will be "belt tightening" at all levels the "haves" as they always have, will survive. Some examples of that first effect can be seen in these figures from some recent purchases of my own: dry lentils (poor man's food) sold at 79¢ a one-pound bag prior to the pandemic; now they are $2.19, while a beef eye-round roast (rich man's food) that cost $7.99 now sells for $17.99. Among the sundry items, Selsun Blue shampoo (used by rich *and* poor) has gone from $5.99 a bottle to $9.79.

A feeble, inept, and actually dishonest attempt has been made to correct, or at least compensate for the imbalance in relief funds totaling several *trillion* dollars, with more under consideration by Congress. But where is this money coming from? Ultimately, it must come from the very people it is supposed to help in this time of their financial distress, the very people who in "normal" times support the Government (the Government has no real money, and even before the current crisis couldn't afford to pay the interest on its more than twenty-one trillion dollar debt). How can we sustain the many trillions more to be added by the massive amount in relief funds that are so desperately needed? And if income tax is to have any meaning at all, there must be an *income*. Half of America's work pool is jobless; no pay, no tax. The second effect will be that barbaric battle for survival.

Before the pandemic, as prices steadily continued to rise while wages remained relatively static and the interest on saving accounts (for those of us who were lucky enough to save anything) was at a munificent .25%. Friends and acquaintances of mine would hear me reflect whimsically on those days in the 1930s and '40s when it seemed to me, as a boy and then teenager, that so many things cost only a nickel. That included those apples sold on the corners of downtown New York City by middle-aged men in the old, worn out but expensive suits they had worn since those palmier days before the great crash of 1929. There were few people, however, in those latter, grim days, who could spare a nickel for such an extravagance.

Now I wonder if, somewhat similar to Mark Twain, who was born and died under Halley's comet, fate has ordained that I be born at the onset of one great depression and die during another even greater one.

June 14, 2020

Although I thought I had said enough about the current situation in this country, the murder of George Floyd by police officer Derek Chauvin[*] in Minneapolis and its aftermath impels me to go on. Much as the pandemic had eclipsed the even greater though less immediate threat of climate change and all its ominous ramifications, that egregious example of police brutality in Minneapolis has obscured the increasing and alarming threat of the pandemic itself. Meanwhile, Trump continues to "tweet" threatening messages about savage dogs guarding the White House against protesters and echoing Miami police chief Hedley's 1967 pronouncement of "When the looting starts, the shooting starts." Otherwise, with the exception of a lone public address at what was purported to be a meeting with the press, Trump had nothing to say about the pandemonium of public outrage. After excoriating China with scathing condemnations for ten minutes and as reporters began to shout their questions about the current situation and his callous tweets, he simply walked away and

---

[*] After Chauvin, the unreasoning soldier of Napolean I, who was contemptuous of other races and from whom the ideology of chauvinism or of chauvinists derived?

back into the White House. Some say that he now is hiding in the cellars of that august building, surrounded by a body guard of secret service agents.

With regard to looting, unless it is bread that is taken, as was the case with Jean Valjean (as in *Les Miserables*), looting has no place in worthy protests. Vandalism, under certain circumstances, perhaps, but adventitious theft, no. Notable also is the serious disregard for the injunctions of the CDC's guidelines about mitigating the effects of the virus: social distancing and the wearing of facemasks. This undoubtedly will add significantly to the number of Covid-19 cases we will suffer. Notable also is the fact that despite their ultra susceptibility to the Coronavirus African Americans turned out in their thousands to protest the killing of George Floyd, thus underlining their fervor.

As to Trump's threatening to invoke the Insurrection Act (1807) using federal troops to do so, one of these conditions must obtain: the state(s) in question must request federal assistance to put down an actual insurrection, i.e. organized armed rebellion against established political authority; a state ignores or refuses to obey a federal law or mandate (as was the case in the 1960's civil rights violations in the south during the Kennedy and Johnson administrations); or as could be the case today, if the states were unable to control violent protest movements and requested assistance, and finally, to protect federal property. As of this writing, none of these could apply under the present circumstances.

Meanwhile, unlike those of Ian Hay Beith's celebratory account of British soldiers going off to meet their fate in the trenches of the Great War, *our* first hundred thousand victims of the pandemic are already dead, sacrificed to the self-serving ineptitude of the indifferent leader who brings shame to that very title. In this as he has on so many other occasions during his infamous reign (for that is what he has made it) Trump has given the lie to that worthy maxim: Uneasy lies the head that wears the crown. He is unquestionably, hopelessly conscienceless. And now, added to the seemingly invincible scourge of the Coronavirus pandemic we have another tiger by the tail, and we're not taming that tiger, we're riding it.

Elsewhere and on more than one occasion I have written about that redoubtable group of thirty-five mental health professionals who in a letter to *The New York Times* of February 13th, 2017, concluded that President Trump, due to his mental condition, was incapable of discharging the duties of his office. In their own words

> Mr. Trump's speech and actions render him incapable of serving as President. This is not a policy matter at all. It is continuous behavior that the whole country can see that indicates *a specific kind of limitations, or problems in his mind.* So to say that those people who are most expert in human psychology can't comment on it is nonsensical (my italics).

and

> The affliction that has gotten the most play…is a form of narcissism so extreme that it affects a person's ability to function: narcissistic personality disorder. The most current iteration of the *DSM (Diagnostic and Statistical Manual of Mental Disorders)* classifies

> [the disorder] as: A pervasive pattern of grandiosity (in fantasy or behavior), need for admiration, and lack of empathy, beginning in early childhood and present in a variety of contexts.

The article goes on to say that diagnosis would require detection of five of nine traits, which it then lists. In my opinion the President's personality and behavior fits every one of the nine to a "T"(rump). Impeachment failed, but is there another way?

The Twenty-fifth Amendment of the Constitution states that:

> Whenever the Vice President and a majority of either the principal officers of the executive department or of any such body as Congress by law may provide,* transmit to the President *pro tempore* of the Senate and the Speaker of the House of Representatives their written declaration that the President is unable to discharge the powers and duties of his office, the Vice President shall immediately assume the powers and duties of the office as Acting President.

One thinks of Woodrow Wilson and the stroke he suffered after the First World War, and of his wife who it is said held the reins for the remainder of his term. I don't think our current first lady would be up to that, so the office would fall to our almost totally ineffectual Vice President. But if Trump's removal were to become a reality it's not

---

* The congressional option or approach would be more feasible since those cabinet officials are all Trump's hand-picked stooges.

inconceivable that Mike Pence might be seen holding his empty head while running out the back door of the White House, leaving Nancy Pelosi to ascend to the throne. In Wilson's case, his inability to carry on as President, was due to a condition of his brain, his mind. Trump's condition, also of the mind though less tangible, is no less disabling. Wilson finished his term in office, but he didn't do it over the dead bodies of hundreds of thousands of innocent U.S. citizens. There are those who would say, Well, he won't be President much longer; he'll never win the election…. Don't bet on it. He still has about eighty million wrongheaded acolytes out there. Longer? How many more victims must fall prey to his blasphemous ministrations by November, 2020? One can hope that the current protests may lead to a greater movement, one calling for a greater change; a more universal systemic change in our governance, at all levels.

After watching Trump, who had been hunkered in that bunker beneath the White House, stroll across to that church in Lafayette Park, again surrounded by a platoon of secret service bodyguards and with an indifferent bible in hand, I've decided to close with this: Some things, not many, are worthy of repetition; so once again let me leave you with this: Justice without power is helpless; power without justice is tyranny.

July 3, 2020

In the early days of the second World War Madame Chiang Kai-shek, wife of the Geralissimo who with his Chinese Nationalist forces was trying desperately to stem the tide of Japanese invaders, was in Hollywood raising money for her beleaguered country. A handsome woman and one of the celebrated Soong sisters, Mme Chiang spoke eloquently in her fluent English exhorting her audience. In that audience were a number of celebrities in their own right, not the least of whom was the actor John Barrymore, accompanied by his friend and fellow reprobate, Errol Flynn. As she went on with her pleas for donations Barrymore muttered to Flynn, "Dammit, this reminds me; I forgot to send my shirts to the laundry!"[*]

Those were the days of the "Confucius" jokes, as in, Confucius say, Woman who fly (or fry) airplane upside down have crack up, to cite just one lurid example of many. In that heyday of Hollywood, in the 1930s, Asians (Orientals then) played only supporting rôles in the movies,

---

[*] At the time no one did as good a job in laundering and pressing shirts than did the small Chinese laundries, usually found in the basements of low rent buildings. Such small business establishments were commonly referred to as "the Chinks."

usually bad characters; the leads were played by whites. Peter Lorre, who rose to prominence in Fritz Lang's German film *M*, was Doctor No, and in those Charley Chan movies the astute Chinese-Hawaiian sleuth was played, sequentially, by Warner Oland, and Sidney Toler, both Swedes. Times *have* changed, however. Pressure from groups such as the NAACP and ACLU, to include the threat of boycotting sponsors' products and services has raised the status of Afro-Americans from that of the "token" or "quota" negro to the zealous if somewhat tiresome policy of placing them in key TV rôles excessively. Today, B.D. Wong, the notable FBI psychiatrist who appears on Dick Wolf's *Law & Order: SVU* from time to time is the antithesis of those Tong hatchet men, the Chinese criminals who infected New York City's Chinatown in and out of their tunnels over a hundred years ago. Of interest also, in a slightly different sense, back then, when radio ruled the airwaves (the theater of the mind), the Green Hornet's "faithful Japanese servant", Kato, became his "faithful *Filipino* servant" the day after Pearl Harbor. The fact remains, both were his *servants*. The radio characters Amos and Andy, ostensibly black (and stereotypical), both were voiced by white actors. Hattie McDaniel, who won an Oscar for Best Supporting Actress in 1939's *Gone with the Wind*, was not permitted to sit with the other (white) nominees. Those were the days when the 1896 Supreme Court decision of Plessy v Ferguson—separate but equal—still held sway; when other black actors and actresses were mere caricatures—Butterfly McQueen, Stepin Fetchit, Farina—the google-eyed black boy in a Joe E. Brown comedy—and so on, and on. These and other such examples of this diverting and stereotypical badinage that titillated people and was commonly accepted by the dominant white people then, who saw it all as "innocent fun," and who would have been surprised to be labelled as racialists. Truly, this was a day of benign prejudice. "The African Dip" was a favorite at carnivals and on boardwalk midways during the 1930s and until the beginning of the Second War.* After all, they were just having fun (at the expense of the less privileged), as many Afro-Americans continued to curse the hand that had branded them with the mark of Ham. Meanwhile, Frankie Laine came out with another hit record called "Shine," yet another name for Afros.

Those were the days when whites enjoyed their unchallenged superiority, blatantly (in the "Solid South"), or more quietly (in the North and West), complacent in their arrogance and indifference to the grinding injustice and envy, yes, envy, of the Negroes, or people of color, or colored people, or just the colored, or worse; whatever they chose to call them from their unassailable cockbird seats. Intermarriage or merely interrelationships between whites and "others" were anathematized, with marriage actually illegal in some states, such as Virginia. Most Afro-Americans accepted these bans as *pro forma*, unassailable.

And it persisted, less openly, less commonly perhaps, until Donna Shalala's coining of that pestilential social mandate of political correctness. In that cheerful little film

---

* This activity held forth at a stand roughly the size of a shooting gallery. At the far end was a tank of water some four feet deep, across the top of which was a wooden bar. Upon the bar was perched a white man in blackface. If a participant, who, given three baseballs for a small fee, hit a target the bar would be released and the "Negro" would fall into the water. The thrower would receive a prize.

of the late 1940s, *Song of the South*, Uncle Remus was just another latter-day Uncle Tom. At a social event in the late 1950s in Georgia, a man who looked like someone between Rhett Butler and Gaylord Ravenal handed me his card. On the face was his name; on the reverse was printed: Fight Segregation! Take a Nigger Home for Lunch. In the late 1960s, along with other "innocent" divertissements, one of those printed-to-order newspapers bore the headline: BLACKS JOIN SPACE RACE; PREDICT A COON ON THE MOON BY JUNE! Accompanied by "The jig's up!" Over time Aunt Jemima (Hattie McDonald with a "do rag" on her head?) and Uncle Ben were transformed into younger, more attractive figures, including a hint of the Caucasian in their features.* The old minstrel shows now are merely recorded history, and if they are mentioned at all, are just aberrant examples of American culture. More recently we have had President Trump's "Kung Flu," much as in that pandemic of a century ago that killed fifty million people and that though it started in the Allied trenches of the Great War was libelously labelled the "Spanish" flu.

Despite the seemingly successful, though costly due to transmission of the COVID-19 virus, nationwide protests (George Floyd could be considered our modern day Crispus Attucks), today racism continues in quieter, more subtle forms. Antiracism, much like political correctness, cannot be legislated, nor can it be denied to future generations of Americans by "brain washing" children of tender age to control their "unconscious or implicit bias." Rather, as

---

* Now they have vanished completely.

I've written elsewhere,[*] it will expire of its own accord, *ab intra* (from within), when through continued and increasing miscegenation we, all of us on this planet, will be similarly complexioned. I envision a species of *homo sapiens* of similar physiognomy, with mesocephalic heads, and classified in the taxonomy as *homo idem* (man the same). And everyone would have a complexion that could be described as the color of a rich *café au lait*.

But for the foreseeable future, racism won't just disappear like some family spirit at dawn. With many Americans, it will be hidden just below the surface of social propriety (P.C. run amok). It will be there but not expressed so openly if not subtly as it once was. You can't legislate political correctness, no more can you legislate choice or taste or emotion, and taste can be applied not merely to gastronomical choices. *Chacun á son gout*, each to his own taste, or *de gustibus non est disputandum*, no amount of persuasion can succeed in changing a person's taste. Much as the word "gay" lost its original meaning, before the word discrimination acquired its pejorative connotation, its *de*notation was complimentary, as in He is a man of fine discrimination: in selecting any number of things: clothing, food, and not least, friends and associates. Racism cannot be simply washed away, like some flaw, real or perceived, in one's appearance. Unfortunately, until this matter of racism resolves itself, several generations of the offspring of biracial unions will have to cope with living in a virtual no man's land, socially, since their acceptance by either race will be, at the least, uncertain.

---

[*] See *A Sharp Seasoning of Truth; A Comprehensive Commentary in Pursuit of Genuine National Security*; Author House, 2019.

Regrettably, as I write this I hear on TV a know-nothing member of the Great Unwashed, one of President Trump's claque of benighted supporters, shouting "White Power!" and other unprintable profanities and obscenities, from a golf cart somewhere. I can't decide which bothers me more: that noisy golfer's "White Power!" or that more subdued old expression of gratitude, "that's very white of you," or worse, "you're a real white man!"

In coming to an end of this screed I would like to add a more general but important note. I have written about the coincidental occurrence and conflation of disasters and hazards we are enduring, about how the current pandemic has virtually eclipsed the looming finality of life as we know it on this planet due to climate change. In turn that very pandemic has been masked to a significant extent by the protests against police brutality and the injustices of our entire system of law and order. Now, these latter two, COVID-19 and the civil protests, have almost drawn a veil over the face of still another dire threat: that of drug addiction. Although there has been virtually no coverage or reporting over the usual news outlets about that enduring and increasing epidemic, increasingly there have been public service announcements and advisories that make it clear that the problem is growing apace and alarmingly. Truly, as that ancient Chinese curse would have it, we are living in interesting times.

Finally, in my last newsletter I gave you a partial quotation from my namesake, Blaise Pascal: "Justice without power is helpless; power without justice is tyranny." Here's the rest of it: "Unable to make what is just strong, we have made what is strong just." Or as someone less gifted would say: Might makes right!* Our chosen and psychopathic leader is killing people in this country at a genocidal rate. The incidence of cases (and deaths) following the ill-advised "reopening" is skyrocketing.

I'll discuss the dilemma of Hispanic Americans, or Latinos, in a subsequent open letter. As to the November election, it wouldn't surprise me if Joe Biden chose an Afro-American woman as his running mate; possibly the mayor of Atlanta or that of Washington, D.C. And keep in mind what I have said about Trump and that Twenty-fifth Amendment to the Constitution.

---

* A classic and outrageous example of which in modern history is the specious establishment of the State of Israel and its subsequent and barbaric treatment of the Palestinian Arabs, aided and abetted by the United States, for the past three-quarters of a century. Another is what we did to the American Indians during the nineteenth century under the spurious, expansionist banner of Manifest Destiny.

In my second open letter I mentioned how the great pandemic of 1918-22 was given the pejorative and racialist label "Spanish" flu. At that time, before the wholesale immigration by Hispanics into the U.S., the British were still calling Spaniards dagos; in the U.S. they were spics. Today, in this more "enlightened" age we call them Spaniards. Ironically, the Hispanics who flock to the United States and who are subject to racial debasement by President Trump and his xenophobic followers are not truly Spanish, however overwhelmingly their names are. I have spent some time in Spain and I have traveled through South and Central America and can state with certainty that in appearance and behavior, the people of the former are little like those of the latter. And, if geographically Spain were located where Mexico now is found, there would be no immigration problem. None.

The undeniable fact is that beyond our southern border a greater proportion of the inhabitants are not of purely Spanish descent but of native American roots. There was a good deal of interracial breeding between the indigenous inhabitants and their Spanish and Portuguese invaders than took place in the north. There, the European invaders, for such practical reasons as the sexual imperative combined with the relative paucity of white women, did induce fraternization (or should that be sorocization?) especially as the occupiers moved west, but still it was less copious than in the southern part of the Western hemisphere. Clearly, when one considers the treatment accorded the northern Indians by our white ancestors there was little or no interest in true or at least a just integration or any inclination toward racial equality. Because the Iberian conquistadores were accompanied by Catholic missionaries, they were encouraged to marry and their progeny given Spanish names, which have endured through the generations since. For all their rapacious exploitation, those occupiers of more than half the hemisphere brought some social stability to the evolution of those people who today call themselves Hispanics or Latinos. The bulk of the people from the south who seek sanctuary in the United States are almost kith and kin of their northern counterparts, the Indians. And much as in the case of African Americans, in this case what we have done to those counterparts is not a page in our history to which we can point with pride.

Will this issue of racism-cum-immigration ever be resolved? Will Mexico ever pay for that trumpeted wall? Will those 800,000 DACA (Deferred Action for Childhood Arrivals) aspirants be treated fairly? The answers to those questions are still unclear. Probably Congress will do nothing to resolve the dilemma fairly, and in this matter, as in all others, President Trump wants nothing to do with procedures, legality, morality, or protocol. All he wants is action and results in favor of achieving his own objectives.

Clearly, like the Roman god Janus, racism wears different faces to suit the moment.

In regard to the state of affairs we have reached in the current pandemic, our failure to control it as other countries have done, added to our own current pandemic crisis, racism, immigration, and not least the skyrocketing drug epidemic, perhaps we should begin to think of the very real possibility of emigration from the U.S. Although the majority of people in this country tend to be isolationists by nature, and conditioned by arrogant nationalism and "American exceptionalism," reinforced by the geographic isolation of being flanked by two large oceans, a number of sensible, right-minded citizens may have had all they can bear of the ineptitude, indifference, and plain dishonesty which pervades our system of governance. The systemic inequity of wealth distribution, our broken system of jurisprudence, with two and one-half million people in prison, more than all other developed countries combined, our out of control drug epidemic (with less than five percent of the world's population, we consume sixty-five percent of its drugs), our obsession with privately owned firearms and the consequent mass killings, our self-inflicted, disruptive, and enduring problem of racism, and our cultural depravity, which we persist in visiting on the rest of the civilized world; all this, and more, provide sufficient reason to look for an orderly, safe, equitable, and more just place in which to spend what is left of one's life.

New Zealand, Australia, and most humiliating, our next door neighbor, Canada, all have put us to shame by solving their COVID-19 onslaughts. Though there are more who have been successful, I mention these few since they all are English speaking and so would suit such of our mainly monolingual expatriates who would seek such sanctuaries. For those relative few who may have one or more other languages, the non-English speaking countries that have defeated the virus may have more to offer than those I have suggested. I, for one, would choose Portugal or the Trentino Canton of Switzerland, which probably is the most sensible, orderly, and safest country in the world. Alternatively, the inhabitants of Denmark are said to be the happiest people in the world.

Currently, the best selling book in the land has yet to reach the book stalls. Mary L. Trump's *Too Much and Never Enough: How my Family Created the World's Most Dangerous Man*, an exposé or "tell-all" book about her uncle, Donald J. Trump, is due to be published by the end of July, 2020. The author is a psychologist, and one wonders if she is in accord with those other thirty-five psychiatrists, psychologists, sociologists, and analysts of human behavior about whom I wrote in an earlier open letter, all of whom concluded, as early in his term as President as February, 2017, that Donald Trump was unable, due to a serious and chronic mental condition, to properly execute the duties demanded by his office. Mary Trump's book, in which she describes her Uncle Don as "a child trapped in a man's body," combined with John Bolton's recent bestseller, *The Room Where It Happened*, and even more recently, CNN commentator Jim Sciutto's *The Madman Theory: Trump Takes on the World*, coupled with the President's refusal to take the pandemic seriously in favor of the concomitant economic disaster, should put paid to any hope he may still retain of winning a second term of office. Understandably, he will use every means at his disposal to prevent his niece's book from being published.

En fin, the lies Trump has expressed in the matter of those hundred-thousand dollar bounties Russia has offered to the Taliban for each American or British soldier killed in Afghanistan will not avail him when the ultimate truth is known.

In previous open letters, I have discussed the state of current affairs in this country and to a lesser extent, elsewhere. Now my intent is to reemphasize certain matters and to add a few more facts and opinions. Generally speaking, the areas I have addressed are the rampant pandemic that is besieging our country; racism and the protests arising from it; the national economic situation; and the drug epidemic that is sweeping the country. These crises, though they may be examined individually, all are interwoven and must be addressed accordingly.

With regard to the COVID-19 menace (along with other deadly serious issues with which we are faced), we must accept the fact that our President is mentally deranged; only those who are similarly afflicted would disagree. Although Trump (and many others) are too ready to tell the world how great we are, this is one occasion when I don't hear very many of their noisy proclamations. Our record in this pandemic scourge doesn't give us anything to boast about. We now lead all other countries in the number of cases and concomitant fatalities due to the virus that is rampaging throughout the land. In fact, we're shattering all kinds of records, such as 70,000 to 80,000 cases of the virus in one day. We always claim to be the best, but in this case (along with many others) aren't we merely the best at being the absolute worst?

To complicate matters, we have become a country of grievously obese, tattooed, body-pierced, look at me!, monkey see, monkey do, self-serving, drug-ridden, wealth worshiping, ill-educated, semi-literate*, immature, ill-mannered, xenophobic, arrogant bullies. We're obsessed by the physical aspects of life, besotted with love of spectator sports (now at our own peril). While all other countries are passionate about their football (soccer to us) we must have all of them. And we have become a nation of contradictions. We fine people who don't use seat belts in automobiles while we only mourn them when they become victims of that peculiarly American obsession with firearms. Our laws (or the lack of them) aid, if not actually abet, the murder of hundreds if not thousands of innocent people annually by mass killings. The U.S. populace can be compared to children who are given lethal weapons and then left to their own devices. And not least we have those other weapons, those that could destroy what's left of this planet, our only sanctuary. What obeisance the rest of the world still shows us is not due to our greatness (in the best sense), and certainly not to our democratic benevolence, but rather to fear of our nuclear arsenal and its potential employment by madmen such as Trump, who are in a position to unleash those weapons of mass destruction without rational consideration.

---

* Nearly thirty percent of U.S. citizens are functionally illiterate (can't read a cooking recipe or instructions for a medication with comprehension). Ten percent are totally illiterate.

As to democratic benevolence, we have made the term oxymoronic. We have evolved a system of governance that does not work, except for a privileged few. That system can be described as democratic capitalism, which because of that deadly sin Avarice Thomas Aquinas spoke of eight centuries ago, will never work.

The issues I have discussed in those previous open letters have one thing in common, and that is division. And it is that dualistic, socio-political polarization, in great part inspired and nurtured by President Trump, that makes us virtually helpless in dealing with today's threats to our very essence and future as a cohesive, equitable nation. The two sides of popular division negate each other, so as to cancel any result but deadlock. Thus we are virtually helpless in dealing with today's threats to maintaining our very fabric as a national entity.

What is needed to rid ourselves of this deadlock are common goals such as that time worn but still valid dedication to life, liberty, and the pursuit of happiness. And to achieve those goals we must have true leadership, from the highest federal level down through the States and local government. We must have social trust in an authoritarian, but enlightened, benevolent system of governance. If we are to defeat this horrific viral invasion there must be rules, and the enforcement of those rules or edicts, mandates, call them what you will, from the very top, not mere suggestions and delegation to the States or even lower levels of governance, but orders whose disregard is punishable by penalties such as fines or in extreme cases even imprisonment. Those countries that have succeeded in their battles with the COVID-19 threat must by now see us, at the very least, as a nation of unruly fools and, at worst, collectively mad and even suicidal in our seemingly docile acceptance of the ravages that continue to kill our citizens by the hundreds *daily*[*]. They also must wonder that this situation exists despite the fact that we boast of having if not the best medical science community in the world, certainly one ranked at the very top.

As to the impact of the pandemic on Trump's vaunted, self-proclaimed successes on the economic front he did himself no favors. His almost frantic insistence on "opening the country" was ill-timed and consequently counter-productive. The end result has been seen by even the most faithful of his stubbornly wrong-headed followers. The staggering rise in the number of cases, hospitalizations, and deaths is enough to convince anyone that "opening the country" so soon led to an absolute disaster in states such as California, Texas, Arizona, and especially Florida, whose governor's lips are inextricably sewn to the President's *derriere*. The enormity of Trump's selfish, depraved act will be seen in the final count of fatalities when the lives of hundreds of thousands of innocent people will have been forfeited in Trump's desperate and vain attempt to get the

---

[*] Although almost 150,000 people have died of the virus since February, a significant number of Americans seem indifferent to this appalling statistic. Has TV, with its gratuitous violence, it's almost pro forma and graphic depictions of killing people, both good and bad, desensitized, dehumanized us as to the value of human life? Whatever the answer, undertakers must be doing a land office business, if you'll permit me to resurrect a dead metaphor. Here and there throughout the country there ought to be seen refrigerated long-haul trailers which contain the corpses that have exceeded the capacity of the hospital morgues. Yes, the mortuaries are thriving; you won't find any unemployment there.

economy back on its feet in order to help him achieve that second term he so ardently desires.

Clearly, such a man must be judged incapable of executing his duties, selflessly, justly, and for the greater good of his people, as President. But judgement is not enough. As in one of the basic tenets of propaganda, an attitudinal change without subsequent behavioral and complementary change is meaningless. The polls are beginning to show that there has been an attitudinal change toward Trump's inadequacies, even among his staunchest, however misguided acolytes. What is needed now is action to reflect and give tangible meaning to that change. Other than the hope that Trump will be voted out of office in November, and despite all his corrupt and harmful record, we have no certain assurance that he will lose the election. We must act, somehow. Need I mention that Twenty-fifth Amendment once more?

In the 1958 film *The Defiant Ones*, Tony Curtis and Sidney Poitier, while chained together, escape from a prison in the deep South. When they are captured by a mob of villagers and told they were going to be lynched, Curtis exclaims indignantly, "You can't hang *me*! I'm a *white* man!" Now, when introducing that vintage film on TV a young man cautions viewers that Curtis' first spoken line in the movie contains the "N" word. He was almost apologetic. No one would have understood this in 1958. Although the word was not used in common parlance then, no one who did use it was censured and those who heard it were indifferent rather than scandalized. After all, the last (known) lynching of a black man occurred a mere eight years prior to the appearance of that film. Between 1877 and that last lynching, 4,400 other Afro-Americans were hanged, a significant number of them for merely smiling "inappropriately" at a white woman.

In 1968, George Wallace, a bigot and confirmed racist who then was the governor of Alabama, made a bid for President of the United States. During that time a morbid joke was circulating which seemed to appeal to most people, both racist and liberal non-racists alike. It seems that Wallace, confined to a wheelchair by now as the gunshot victim of an assassination attempt, received a telephone call from his doctor who had recently run some tests on the governor during a routine physical examination. "I have some news for you Governor, some good and some bad," he announced without preamble. "Give me the good news first, Doc" Wallace replied. "Well," went on the other, "I'm afraid you've got only six months to live, George, maybe less." "Jesus H. Christ!" came back Wallace. "That's the *good* news? What the hell's the bad news?" and heard, "The bad news is that you're dying of sickle cell anemia."*

Racism does indeed take many forms and time changes the forms it will take, but the salient and undeniable truth is that the ethos of white supremacy continues in some form or other and will endure until the changes in social mores blur the differences in physical appearance between whites and people of color. Until then those

---

* A disease that afflicts Africans almost exclusively, much as the dreaded Tay-Sachs disease affects Jews. Today, just mentioning those fatal illnesses in connection with the races that are prone to suffer them is considered politically incorrect. Now we know that the Afros, for a number of reasons but not least physiological ones, are significantly more susceptible to the Corona Virus.

people of color, however earnestly they strive to achieve equality, will have to content themselves with the results of any pressures they can bring to bear to ameliorate their social status. Meanwhile their frustration and bitterness can only be imagined, while evoking images of Fats Waller singing "Black and Blue," Toni Morrison, as a girl, literally praying that she might have blue eyes, and Michael Jackson trying by any conceivable means to look like a white man.

But however much pressure activist organizations such as the NAACP and ACLU bring to bear to further their objectives, prejudice will continue. The threatened boycotting of sponsors' products and services as advertised on TV unless more equality was given to actors and actresses of color, in commercials as well as standard programming, is an example of such pressure. But one clear indicator of this continuing prejudice lies in the fact that those "outsiders" who have been given more prominent rôles still are chosen in large part for their closer resemblance to Caucasian standards of "good looks." That short-lived "Black is Beautiful" slogan of the 1960s was a feeble and forlorn attempt to "level the playing field." Today's "Black Lives Matter" makes much more sense. The women especially are those who, at least physically, display features and traits that Caucasians have established and accepted as the standard for physical beauty—high cheek bones, refined noses (some with a slight uplift), "round" eyes, abundant but silken hair without receding hairlines, lips, sensuous but not overly generous, and so on. Watch TV's CNN for a panoply of young white women who set the standard. Representative of this for Afros, Hispanics, and Asians in that order we have:

Lena Horne (of *Cabin in the Sky* fame), Anacani[*] (of the *Lawrence Welk* ménage), and Nancy Kwan (*Flower Drum Song*). Somewhat ironically, there can be little doubt that in each case there was a generous amount of Caucasian in each woman's ancestry. Among the men Harry Belafonte, Shemar Moore, and "The Rock," Dwayne Johnson provide good examples of the Afros while Fernando Lamas (You're mahvelous, dolling), or Antonio Banderas and Jimmy Shigeta (*Flower Drum Song*) will serve for the Hispanic and Asian males, respectively. Most recently, in this time of socio-political protests and demonstrations activists have declared a "Blackout Day," enjoining Afro-Americans to refrain from spending any money, personally or online, in a day-long boycott. The activists claim that Afro-Americans spend a trillion dollars a year on products and services.

As to the protests themselves which have continued since the murder of George Floyd, and as a comment on the incompetence and ineptitude of our entire system of law and order, suffice it to say that, added to the xenophobia that exists among many Americans, and the fact that at least half our young men are "gun happy," I have only this to say. While the candidates for entering the police forces of European countries must undergo, on average, two years of training and complete the course successfully, here in the United States the time spent in those "academies" we hear so much about on those TV police procedurals, again, on average, is a mere twenty weeks.

---

[*] Whose full name is Anacani Maria Consuelo y Castillo Lopez Cantor Montoya. You can't get any more Spanish (read Caucasian), to include that Jewish "Cantor".

Meanwhile, the drug epidemic continues to rage throughout the country unabated. Reduced to its simplest terms and stated as the first principal of that dismal science, economics, it's a matter of supply and demand. Our government tries almost desperately to place the blame for our affliction of drug addiction anywhere except where it truly belongs. It's those drug runners from Mexico, we hear, or it's those growers in Columbia; it's the drug dealers in our very country; it's the ease with which too many doctors reach for their prescription pads (not the ease and alacrity with which the big pharmaceutical houses fill the orders and distribute the drugs?), and so forth.

As to that last excuse, there is another more subtle epidemic seeping through our populace. "Depression" now has become more than just a household word and can be found throughout the medical literature—in diagnostic tracts of course, but now even in medical background questionnaires to be filled out by the patient. "Are you depressed?" or other forms of the question are to be found along with those other routine questions we all are familiar with. Antidepressants now are the third most prescribed medication in the world. Perhaps if those people who suffer from depression had lived through a real depression such as the Great one of the 1930s, their problems, real or perceived, might seem lighter.

But back to that age-old economic principal of Supply and Demand. Let us accept the fact that it is mainly demand that is driving our drug problem to reach unmanageable proportions, and as long as there exists that unquenchable demand there will be no end of suppliers to satisfy its need. As Al Capone said about illicit alcohol during those crime-ridden days of Prohibition, "I just give 'em what they want. If they didn't want it, I'd be out of business this afternoon. Hell, they'll always want it."

This just in. In company with Great Britain, Australia, and Canada, we're now claiming that the search for an anti-virus vaccine has been hacked by unknown sources or possibly some nation-state such as Russia. The hacker goes by the name of Cozy Bear. If it's another nation, rather than keep the data secret we should share it with them, not fight over it. We're *all* in this frightful onslaught together. As to the vaccine *per se*, we must not be foolishly hopeful. The fact that Phase III testing has already begun is no guarantee that in a mere six months medical scientists will have developed an effective and safe vaccine. Meanwhile, all we can and *must* do is try to mitigate this satanic scourge by what means we have available: going back, as a cohesive nation, not merely a hodgepodge of states making the process up as they go along, to a national shutdown, going back to square one of that CDC plan to "reopen the nation," with all its tiresome and frustrating rules. We must shut down again, as a nation, but this time with strict enforcement of those rules. Meanwhile, we can only hope that, almost miraculously, a suitable vaccine becomes available[*].

Almost as critical to the situation is the matter of testing. Since the World Health Organization declared the Coronavirus a pandemic our feeble and inefficient efforts in testing have failed completely. As early as late January we refused to accept a testing system offered us by German

---

[*] Meanwhile, Trump and his disreputable dummy Peter Navarro continued to tout Hydroxychloroquine as a therapeutic drug to treat the virus. Navarro crows "I've got tens of millions of tablets in the national stockpile." Has Trump invested heavily in this drug that his own scientists have discredited?

scientists in Berlin, declaring (President Trump) that only a test developed in the U.S. would do (more American "exceptionalism"). So our CDC came up with a test, which proved to be a complete failure. In our arrogance, our efforts in adequate and effective testing have failed so completely as to make us a laughing stock on a global scale. In regard to the timeliness in obtaining the results of what testing we do, inadequate as it may be, if such a catastrophe were not so dire, one could say, in jest, that people are apt to die of old age before their test results become available to them. They should get them before they leave the test site, and, not least, the tests should be free. And on the matter of medical bills, who is to pay for the millions of patients who are being hospitalized and require some of the costliest care necessary, often critical to any chance of their survival. This is true especially now when unemployment is rife and many people can't even afford housing and are being evicted, increasingly, daily. More financial aid will be needed, immeasurably more, to make up the deficits which must be incurred by the entire medical community if they are to continue with their heroic endeavors. But ultimately, our children, and even their children, if we even survive this two edge sword of Damocles which hangs above us. And those hospitals and medical attendants will want payment. After all, this is a *capitalist* democracy.

Meanwhile, that virus relief bill continues stalled in the Congress, mainly due to the Senate's moving at its accustomed glacial speed. And when the people of that top one percent of the wealth charts start buying gold it might be a good idea to keep an eye on the Stock Market. Keep an eye also on those paramilitary Homeland Security troops

Trump is sending into cities with Democrat mayors to quell "the unruly protesters." It's difficult, for this observer at least, not to recall those brutal thugs called his Brown Shirts that Hitler sent into German towns and cities in the early and mid 1930s to "quell" *his* detractors.

August 6, 2020

So the virus continues to spread, and none of the best medico-scientific minds on the planet can predict with any certitude where it will take us. Will we ever be completely rid of this modern day plague? We don't know. As to the disease itself one disturbing fact is emerging: those who have contracted it and have "recovered" may never be completely "out of the woods." Medical investigation has revealed that this latter day pestilence, in many if not all cases, will have a lingering effect. Aside from hair loss, strokes, permanent damage to the lungs, kidneys, liver, and not least the heart, the virus will result, in varying degree, in more subtle physical limitations to the victim. That is to say, certain athletes who seem to have recovered fully will find they no longer can hit a pitched ball as well as they once could, or make that double play; quarterbacks will no longer be able to throw a pass as far or as accurately as they once could; basketball players no longer will be able to jump as high; or, in a totally different form of physical activity, professional dancers will find that certain steps they once performed easily now have become impossible to execute. And again, we don't know why. Even more troubling is the fact that it is highly probable that proper testing will show that we may have *ten times* or more cases than the numbers now reveal, i.e., about *fifty million* infected people.

Yes, the virus continues to spread, and in some parts of the globe is even resurging. Germany is one example. There are 34,674 members of our armed forces stationed in Germany, of the 63,631 throughout Europe. Although there may be restrictions imposed on civilian travel between Europe and the U.S., I've heard of no such restrictions placed upon "our ambassadors of good will" and their dependents. If such is the case, and considering the great number of uniformed Americans who travel continuously between the two hemispheres and elsewhere—on ordinary or emergency leave, as replacements, as medevacs, on official business— what are the odds, considering the horrific number of cases and deaths here in the U.S., on our contributing to that resurgence in Germany? And, with our 700 bases— army, navy, and air force—throughout the world, with a total of 170,000 personnel, excluding their accompanying dependent families, where else might we have taken that virus?

One of the salient matters addressed in this series of open letters concerns President Trump and his bizarre approach to and his total mismanagement of the COVID-19 crisis. Among his deceits, delays, deferments, diversions, deflections and distractions resulting from his paranoidal, narcissistic lunacies, he has continued to excoriate and accuse other nations, individuals, and even the World Health Organization as to the inception of the virus and their attempts to defeat it. Recently I watched on TV as a senior Indonesian diplomat was asked who was to blame for the origins of the pandemic and its persistent threat to mankind. Without hesitation he replied, and I paraphrase: "You know, I think of a group of people on a ship at sea that has caught fire. They are arguing hotly about how the fire started, until someone says sensibly, 'Why don't we put out the fire first and then we can argue about who started it.'"

But we have already discussed, *passim*, Trump's gross mismanagement of the crisis and its probable consequences. More and more voices are being heard in acknowledgement of his failures, not least on TV where we hear, almost *ad nauseum* now, about his mistakes and failures and where they are leading us. But what are the realities and fundamental causes of his disastrous behavior? And as important, what should we do, what *can* we do about it?

In former, more forthright times, before the wave of social timidity we call political correctness (in its truly *political* sense) produced a society of milquetoast muddlers, and before the advent of straitjackets, a person displaying the symptoms manifest in President Trump would have been wrapped up in a wet sheet and trundled off to the nearest looney bin. Prior to that, in even more rustic but straightforward times, he would have had a large net cast over him and been consigned to an *oubliette*[*] until he starved to death or managed somehow to kill himself. In Trump's case and in these mealy-mouthed and too forgiving times all I can do, as I have said several times, is to call your attention to that Twenty-fifth Amendment to our Constitution.

As Steve McQueen said in the movie *The Sand Pebbles* (1966) when his Chinese friend was being flayed to death in plain sight by a thousand cuts and while his American gunboat Captain dithered—"Well, do *somethin'*!"

---

[*] A dungeon with an opening only at the top (as in a common well).

August 16, 2020

Please take this in the same spirit in which it is offered. With still eighty days to go before the presidential election, we're being suffocated with news about civil rights, social injustice, and the inequities of our judicial system, in short, the inequity between whites and "people of color." Afro-Americans especially have achieved a never before prominence on TV—on the news outlets, entertainment programs, and not least in commercials. Recently, Joe Biden's selection of Kamala Harris, the daughter of Indian (as in New Delhi) and Jamaican parents, as his running mate has given even more impetus to this. All well and good—up to a point. As is said of fertilizers, a little makes the grass green, but too much kills it. Now, Beth Gayle, widow of Tyrone Gayle, former secretary to Kamala Harris, has appeared on CNN. Beth Gayle is the quintessential "girl next door," a young, blond, pretty, fresh-complexioned white woman. Her late husband, who died of cancer recently, was black.

If the Democrats keep pushing all this into prominence, we might see a backlash, an overload of the grid, as the power providers would say. Every racist or white supremacist, open or "closet," will crawl if needs must to the polling station to cast his or her vote for Donald Trump. And if Trump wins his cherished second term we well might see a resurgence of those Jim Crow days, socially, and our small children and grandchildren will be reading Helen Bannerman's *Little Black Sambo* (1899) in school again (as did I). And Americans will continue to die from the COVID-19 virus (as have the more than 900 public health workers) at the rate of one per minute.

We must hope that Trump's frenetic efforts to derail the electors' mail-in voting will fail to his cost. But though he may be mentally unbalanced, Trump is not stupid. Using our archaic, flawed Electoral College system* to support his objective, he will make every effort to delegitimize, derail, in short sabotage the election by suppressing voting. If there were no Electoral College and the presidency were decided by simply the popular vote he knows he wouldn't stand a chance. He knows also that because of the pandemic and their fear of being infected at the polling places many people would use the system of mail-in-voting. But under the Trump appointed Postmaster General, Lewis DeJoy, himself under investigation by the Inspector General for his business connections with Amazon, one of the U.S. Postal Service's largest accounts, all possible assistance is being given the President—mailboxes are being removed in the hundreds, high speed sorting machines are being deactivated or destroyed, closing times for post offices

---

* What we need is a Constitutional Convention, where in addition to ridding ourselves of that misbegotten Electoral College, we could address, clarify, and change the Constitution to better suit the times and settle certain matters such as that controversial Second Amendment and the inequitable apportionment of Senators (based on the population of each State). c.f. the Twelfth and Twenty-third Amendments to the Constitution.

have been reestablished at twelve noon, overtime pay no longer is permitted, and generally shaving operations in any conceivable way in order to suppress mail-in voting. Meanwhile, Trump is doing his utmost to ensure that Congress withhold the funds the postal service needs to handle the massive number of mail-in ballots. If these measures are successful the election would be in pandemonium with controversy over who won lasting for weeks if not months, during which time Trump would remain in office to continue his evil doings. So the voter is left with a sort of Hobson's Choice: Go to the polling station and risk contagion, and possibly death, or stay home, mail your vote in, and hope it will be counted.

If he hadn't caused so much havoc and its attendant grief, Trump's megalomania would provide a source of endless entertainment for the entire nation instead of one of pain and irreparable damage. In going through the archives of my globetrotting days, I came across a photo of myself in an old international driver's license. In a frivolous moment of *diablerie*, I transposed that head and shoulders photo to a postcard picture of Mt. Rushmore, to replace that huge bust of George Washington. I must admit that the substitution was a complete success in size, shading, and even background. Then I sent copies of this *coup de theatre* to a few friends, whose reactions ranged from one who expressed a doubtful reserve at my thoughtless presumption (he isn't the brightest bulb in the chandelier and had little or no sense of humor), to absolute hilarity on the part of the rest. But recently I had to concede that I had been trumped by the man himself (no, not George, Donald!). Although the President denied any knowledge that the White House staffers had asked, seriously, the Governor of South Dakota if she would agree to the emplacement of a bust of Trump to join that small pantheon of former presidents in the massive sculpture on Mt. Rushmore it is entirely probable that it was he who inspired the overture in the first place.

Having mentioned George Washington, one wonders whether, along with taking down all those Confederate generals who fought bravely to preserve slavery, as well as replacing their names on the entrances to all those posts, camps, and stations in the South, others might qualify for a similar fate. Both Washington and Jefferson kept slaves; the latter even propagated one or two. Lincoln's in-laws had slaves. Can we envision the statues, monuments, and memorials of those illustrious leaders being torn down? Only for chronological reasons would Teddy Roosevelt survive, and there'd be plenty of room for Trump to join him.* Would we have to demolish the memorials of Jefferson and Lincoln in the national's capital? Would the Washington monument be brought down by controlled demolition? (perhaps as an added attraction at the next Independence Day celebration in Washington, which itself would have to be renamed.) Taking Washington as our prime example, would that last imperative follow logically if we took just *one* statue of him down? Today that is a reasonable question;

---

* Trump would be in good company alongside the man who put his own name forward to receive the Medal of Honor, awarded for conspicuous gallantry and the nation's highest award, for his service in Cuba during the Spanish-American War. This included his participation in the Battle of San Juan Hill, considered by all *honest* students of military history to have been a disaster for the U.S. forces there. The Thirteenth Amendment (Emancipation Proclamation) would spare his removal from Mt. Rushmore, at least for now.

before the advent of our current president it would have been considered an outrage.

As to Trump's proclivity for poking barbs into his enemies, real or just perceived, and apropos of his slandering Kamala Harris, his unmistakable illiteracy (Yosemight National Park, Thighland) will deny him this: in the mid-eighteenth century Samuel Richardson published a sentimental book entitled *Pamela*, which was followed by a satirical spoof called *Shamela* by Henry Fielding. Pamela was a hit.

An open letter, yes, but a directed one; directed at those of you who have some influence to do something to get us out of this slough of despond we have blundered into. You talk, talk, talk endlessly and repetitiously about our dilemma, but don't do anything to resolve the problem at its root causes, and the all too obvious solutions, as the death toll continues to rise exponentially, with more than 170,000 already dead, millions of jobs lost, thousands of small businesses closed, many never to reopen, and still counting. Many small businesses insured themselves against business interruptions (such as natural hazards, but does that include pandemics?). Now, insurance companies can't or won't meet the bill—about a trillion dollars—so where's the money to come from? What to do? I don't travel through the world as I once did, undoubtedly I will spend what time I have left here in the U.S. until I go on that last great adventure. This relieves me of having to encounter people in foreign nations, which once was informative and often pleasing. Today I would feel humiliated to admit to them that I was a citizen of the United States (unhappily, we are fast losing the right to use that word "united").

But why are we waiting, and hoping, to rid ourselves of the malefactor and principal cause of our afflictions by means of the coming election? Yes, hoping, since we have no assurance that he will be beaten by Biden and company. What if there were to be no presidential election on November third? There are those who will say, Oh well, the election is just a couple of months away, we'll get rid of him then.… Well and good, but how many more unnecessary deaths are we willing to endure? Are we standing that old aphorism on its head: Don't just do something, stand there—with five and one-half million cases, more than 173,000 dead, thirty million people out of work, tens of thousands of small businesses closed, and, not least, humiliating ourselves in the face of the world? Is that not enough to demand and justify *some* action *now*. Meanwhile, to paraphrase an old line*, Trump golfs while America disintegrates. Clearly, President Trump is a psychopath, one could say even more definitively that he is a sociopath. This is not merely my opinion, but has been attested to during his term in office by several dozen highly qualified professionals in the science of human psychology. As early as February 2, 2017, in a letter to *The New York Times*, a group of thirty-five of those professionals concluded that

> Mr. Trump's speech and actions make him incapable of serving as president.…The affliction…is a form of narcissism so extreme that it affects a person's ability to function: narcissistic personality disorder.

---

* Nero fiddles while Rome burns.

and in the interim Trump has done nothing to disprove this diagnosis. *Au contraire*, he has provided the American public living proof that it is true and just by his speech and actions. So what has everyone been waiting for? Could it be that other failed attempts such as the Mueller Report and more latterly his attempted removal by impeachment make us hesitate? Why don't those so-called representatives of ours in Washington stop dithering and bring that Twenty-fifth Amendment I have alluded to in several of these open letters into the daylight? With enough popular opinion generated it just might work. As I've also said before, an attitudinal change is only that; what makes things move is a behavioral change that takes advantage of that change in attitude. Why don't we jettison all the temerity and ineffectual iterations and reiteration of what that self-serving madman is doing to this country and frog-march him out of the White House? We've done pretty well protesting police brutality; why don't we see what we can do about protesting the president's behavior? Trump's actions (or inaction) have made police behavior look petty by comparison. The unnecessary deaths he has been responsible for, however indirectly, put him in a class all his own. It is only fair to add, however, that his depredations were made easier owing to the fact that, as a class, Americans are somewhat ignorant, immature, and unruly. As is said among comedians, he's had a great audience to play to.

Finally, but not of least importance, is that if Trump does lose the election, he will use every means available to him to protest the outcome, resulting in what could mean months of adjudication and arbitration before a final resolution is reached; and during that tumultuous time, the pandemic will rage on with even more disastrous results.

With what has been said already in the first series of open letters as a point of departure, let us now begin to examine some of the deeper and basic faults and systemic failings in our system of capitalist democracy and the exercise of its governance. Taking it in parts, let's begin with what can be called a peculiarly American obsession.

I think it would be appropriate to say at the outset that having spent more than twenty years as an infantryman in our Army, with one assignment as head of all light and heavy weapons training at a U.S. infantry center, I am not unacquainted with firearms, their use, and their effect. Though fortunately my experience with and use of weapons has always been "lawful", I have had serious misgivings about what I was involved in after seeing what effect they can have on human beings. There were many times, as in Vietnam, when I wished there could have been another way...

But let me go on from a tragedy on foreign shores to a somewhat similar tragedy in our own country. Aside from their seemingly compulsive tendency to lard their language with excessive prepositions* Americans seem possessed by another less benign and, in proven fact, much more lethal obsession.

Pervading much of rural America is a fascination about firearms, and its inevitable consequences follow: sprees, "road rage," mass shootings, and other anti-social gun violence. (Significantly if more benignly, in rural America today it is almost impossible to find a traffic sign without bullet or pellet holes.) Urban gun violence occurs mainly for more tangible reasons: adversarial gang violence, robbery connected homicides, domestic violence, and so on. In the former case what once was known as the Wild West played its part. All those "Westerns," the so-called "oaters" or "horse operas," played their part. Beginning in 1896, they were a major and lucrative part of the movie mega-industry as it is today. The virtual deification of such low-life characters as the James brothers and Billie the Kid (the whoreson young back shooter Henry McCarty, from Brooklyn, New York who went West seeking adventure). In at least one sense John Wayne, much honored as one of America's greatest heroes, at least fictionally, has done as much of a disservice to the people of the United States as any of its greatest traitors who may come to mind—and there have been a number of them, not all of whom are considered as such.

---

* When I leave an airplane that has landed, I get off, not off *of* the plane. Similarly, I want *for* you to (something). To say, "continue *on*," is like saying, Not only is it perforated, but it's got holes in it. What else could one do, if one decided to continue? And when a preposition begs to be used, it is ignored. We no longer "cave *in*," we merely "cave"; we don't bail *out*, we just bail (from the airborne to the navy, in one short phrase), and we don't shop *at* The Salmon Run Mall, we just shop it—chancy, since one meaning of "shop' is to betray.

The naming of such towns as "Cut and Shoot" and "Point Blank" (both in Texas—where else?) do not inspire one to a sense of Arcadian peace and tranquility, but merely add to this puerile, though dangerous, impulse.

With this obsession has come a calloused indifference, an acceptance of the tragedies that accompany this runaway epidemic of small arms shootings. While listening to the local news in Baltimore years ago I heard the replay of a 911 call in which the caller, when asked, "What is the problem, sir?" responded in a tone more indignant and irritated than agitated and grief-stricken with "Hey! They just shot my fuckin' girlfriend!" He might as well have been saying, "Damn it! My car just broke down."

What *is* this fascination, accompanied by the equally dangerous insouciance, exemplified by that 911 caller, with firearms all about, anyway? To better feed and satisfy this fascination with firearms, producers of television shows and motion pictures with their virtually formulaic violence have crammed every conceivable small arms weapon and increasingly, some not so small: hand-held rocket or grenade launchers, semi- or fully automatic cannon, even ground-to-air missile launchers onto our viewing screens. Ironically, while Americans celebrate violence, the majority of them are too timorous to engage in it.

Beyond all this "militarization" of civilian activity is the increasing tendency toward the "benign" representation of matters military in the commercial and public service sphere of television. We see a mother who proudly tells us that during her pregnancy she and her fetus were "warriors," defending bravely against her cancer; a fat caricature of a general in full uniform roars about in a fast car, while selling insurance; a man wearing goggles and a protective HAZMAT coverall is seen cleaning out a cat's litter box using a spray device that looks very much like a machine pistol. At a Colts-Bills football game the announcer says something about giving your "unit" a chance to succeed. Not team, club, or organization, but unit, as in one's company, battalion, regiment, etc. A TV commercial for a university of doubtful provenance announces: "(NHSU) University can change the entire trajectory of your life." "Trajectory," as in the parabolic flight of an artillery shell, for course, path, or arc.

As if we didn't already suffer enough from an overabundance of cliché, we now have a new lexicon of synonyms that, once common mainly among members of the military and police, now have become prominent in the public domain. "Special Forces flashlights" are touted (they never gave *me* one). Another flashlight, advertised as a "Battle Light with Atomic Beam." A Tac Vision device replaces sun visors in cars, used to cut down the glare of the sun or approaching headlights, and Battle or Night Vision Tac(tical) sunglasses. A medication for acne is a "secret weapon." And why has camouflaged clothing come into vogue for civilian wear? The last gratuitous lens-cleaning cloth I received from an optometrist with my new glasses also is in camouflage color and design. Are the civilians playing soldier on a safe parade ground?* Also, college dorms now are residence halls. Will it end as "barracks"? (But of course a toilet is still a bathroom.) We sell products with

---

* A suitable bumper sticker, in red, white, and blue, might be, **Thank You For Your Service!-I'll Wait For You Here**. Meanwhile, the Infantry Officers Training Center at Fort Benning, Georgia maintains its inspirational motto of, **Follow Me!**

names such as not simply two-sided tape but *Tiger* tape, and not just strong or hold-fast glue, but *Gorilla* Glue. Recently, the TV hucksters have been touting Airborne Gummies. Surely they might consider such evocative names or slogans as Special Ops Sugar Pops, Rollos, or Reese's Rangers, Seal Team Creams, or Sugar Babies, or Daddies? I offer all these freely and gratuitously for their consideration. There will be more; look for them.

I have read that every other house in America has at least one firearm. There now are more than 320 million firearms in civilian hands in this country (one for every man, woman, and child), with three million more being produced each year. While here in the U.S. there were 33,000 gunshot deaths in 2016, 2017 outdid that figure by an appalling three percent. There are less than 200 deaths attributed to gun violence in the other 200 nations throughout the world. The United Kingdom, perhaps our closest ally (along with of course Israel, which claims that honor in the Middle East), sustained merely 143. During a spate, or spree if you will, over just a few weeks in the Fall of 2017, we sustained 26 dead in Texas, 49 in Miami, and 59 dead and 515 wounded in Las Vegas, which will almost certainly cause the body count to go over 33,000 for 2017. Gunshot deaths probably will surpass America's other killer preoccupation, auto accident fatalities. Trauma centers in urban areas are being forced to close because they can't afford the cost of treating, free, so many indigent gunshot victims; so they won't be there to treat victims of auto accidents or other serious "legitimate" injuries. Currently, in late 2020, we are sustaining over one hundred gunshot fatalities per day.

Consider now the situation that exists and almost daily becomes more volatile and deadly on both sides of our border with Mexico. Can the American "Gringos," as those Mexican drug runners know us, complain about the horrors being committed in Mexico and within our own border with that country? Whom can we blame when while comprising less than five percent of the world's population, we account for between 35 and 65 percent (figures vary widely between U.S. Government and other, less biased, authorities) of the consumption of illegal drugs? Added to that and more to the point of this writing, should the blatant and freebooting sale and shipment of firearms of all kinds by U.S. gun dealers, with the tacit approval of the government's Alcohol, Tobacco, Firearms (ATF) (and now, "Explosives"), Bureau, to those same "drug cartels" be countenanced by any right-thinking U.S. citizen?

Advocates in this country of the right of individuals to keep and bear arms under the aegis of the Second Amendment to our Constitution, though they may not be pleased about it, apparently are willing to tolerate all this, or at least accept the too often tragic consequences of this right. But just what does that now controversial Second Amendment say? It says that "A well regulated militia, being necessary to the security of a free State, the right of the people to keep and bear Arms, shall not be infringed." Why? Because when the Constitution was written the States feared Federal interference in their affairs; oppression, even mandates imposed by the central government.

What *was* the intention of this Amendment in 1791, when the Bill of Rights was ratified? Do the same conditions still apply today? Are these murderous, armed street gangs we read about or hear about every day part of a well-regulated State militia dedicated to preserve the security of their respective sovereign States? Are those sociopaths who regularly shoot indiscriminately into crowds, killing annually *thousands* of men, women, and children a safeguard to states' rights? As the former TV pundit Sam Donaldson would ask whenever he had the opportunity: "Should individuals have the right, under the Second Amendment, to keep bazookas, mortars, howitzers, and other heavy weapons? Should the states, in order to be secure (against whom, the Federal Government?) be allowed to possess nuclear weapons?"

The proposal during the Clinton régime to ban nineteen types of semiautomatic weapons passed the House (by two votes), and that was a step in the right direction, but only a hesitant, tiny step.* We've proven twenty-six times that the Constitution can be amended. Why is it so difficult, in this case, to see that it's time to do it again? The Constitution is human scripture, not holy writ. It wasn't framed with the intention of doing more harm than good, and it contains its own mechanism for the changes the framers knew would become inevitable.

How can we hold ourselves in such high esteem before the rest of the "civilized" world while we are content to

---

* In any case, anyone with more than a passing knowledge of small arms knows that by adjusting or removing an item called a sear, contained in the receiver of such a dual capability weapon, can convert that piece to fully automatic fire. Now another modification called a bump stock will provide almost the same cyclic rate of fire. Such a device was used in the Las Vegas mass killing in October 2017. And, in passing, I wish the supposed experts in all those crime programs on TV would stop referring to the empty cartridge cases found "at the scene" or elsewhere as "shell" casings, as if they were the *disjecta membra* of major artillery or naval ammunition; shotgun ammunition (shells), yes; all other small arms brass, no.

condemn ourselves to living with the highest incidence of murder and every other form of violent crime in that world? What sort of example are we setting for the rest of the world's societies? Meanwhile, Wayne La Pierre and his bullheaded members of the National Rifle Association and their supporters proudly boast that while the rest of the world's "advanced" countries have found it necessary to disarm their private citizens we, after more than 200 years, still maintain, in their ill-conceived boasting, the right to keep and bear firearms! But to what end, and at what cost? Can the puerile joy of a (law abiding) weekend shooter equate with the unimaginable grief, which must be endured, daily, by countless survivors of thousands of gunshot victims—good or bad, guilty or innocent—throughout the land, to say nothing of the fate of the victims themselves? Why is it so difficult for us to act sensibly? Why don't we stop marking time on this vital issue—marching in place—and step off purposefully, in a confident way, toward a constructive, rewarding objective that will relieve the general populace of this persistent scourge?

September 1, 2020

W e have our own, self-inflicted, form of domestic terrorism. Trump and the NRA imply that the only solution lies in defending against armed attacks. Again, not prevention by eliminating the causes, as in the Middle East situation or drug addiction, but something like putting band aids on skin cancer and sending the patient home.[*] There are gun shows and swap meets, and sometimes they are combined affairs. Thirty-seven percent of all gun owners were under eighteen years of age when they bought their first gun(s). Gun distributers such as L.L. Bean and Dick's Sporting Goods now are requiring buyers to be twenty-one years of age and they have stopped selling semi-automatic "long guns"; Florida has changed its laws along the same lines. But a recent convention of NRA gun owners, dutifully attended by President Trump, changed nothing substantially. And modern technology is adding to the problem. However unintentionally, Charles Hull, who invented the 3-D printer, may go down in infamy. A process has evolved whereby anyone with a three dimensional printer can produce a gun with no history—no

---

[*] Or thinking those scabs of impetigo on a child's legs are signs of healing.

registration number. Since they're made of plastic polymers (with exception of the diminutive firing pin) they can't be detected at security check points.

Can we envision a beginning for real and substantive change? Could the states, acting on their own authority, begin a movement to achieve what the greater part of the population wants?* The Democrats don't have guns at the top of their agenda as do the Republicans, who have been so saturated by NRA propaganda that they continue unquestioningly to cry out zealously for "their Second Amendment rights," much like the vast crowds cheering Hitler's every word at those Nürnberg rallies in the 1930s.

Too many times in the last quarter-century or more has a seemingly avid American TV audience watched as a "corpse" lying on an autopsy slab was subjected to the gruesome procedures being carried out. The human body, which once was called in more innocent times generously a vessel of God now is displayed to the public in its grossest, foulest, and most repugnant condition, which is diametrically opposed to the more glorifying aspects of its external appearance (to some) in such elevated mediums as *Sports Illustrated* and a variety of fashion magazines. This dichotomy does nothing more than to confuse, perhaps only subconsciously, but worse in certain cases, to desensitize the viewer, especially the younger ones to a point where the destruction of human life is no vitally important matter, no more than a butcher cutting a pork loin into chops. This artificial, theatrical graphic, but totally gratuitous

---

* As I have suggested elsewhere, what we need is a constitutional convention, where we could resolve this issue as well as rid ourselves of that infernal electoral college and settle other controversial matters.

and unnecessary exercise in "virtual reality" serves only to further desensitize, one could even say dehumanize, the viewer by diluting shocking reality and reducing it to mere entertainment. Actually attending an autopsy performed on a gunshot victim is a totally different experience, especially if the victim is a seven-year-old child who was killed wantonly in a school shooting.

Led and inspired by students who survived that massacre at Parkland, Florida, on 24 March 2018, marches and demonstrations took place in Washington, 800 other cities throughout the country, and even in foreign countries, protesting the U.S. Government's callous indifference to gun regulation. A half-million appeared in Washington to protest. A number of participants carried signs on which was inscribed NRA = (a picture of a tombstone). While these youngsters have put to shame a majority of U.S. adults, both those for or against gun control, what is needed now is what propagandists call a "bandwagon": a well-organized campaign persuading a majority of the populace that if they don't agree with those courageous young people they are out of step with the times and with the current majority position on the question of that archaic Second Amendment "right." The following day the Pope expressed his support of the movement with enthusiasm. Unfortunately my better sense overtook my enthusiasm and I predicted this commendable and exemplary effort by the adolescent would-be victims alone would bear little fruit, as it has.

The Parkland Florida students were exempted from taking the state final exams required before graduation. There were even suggestions that the building where the shooting took place be razed and a new one built. More nonsense; accomplishing nothing, but accepting the shooting as just another one of life's trials.

However, there may still be hope. We may witness a modern-day "Children's Crusade," and I fervently hope this one, unlike its predecessor of the early thirteenth century, doesn't end as an abortive effort, as when 30,000 French and German youngsters attempted to join their elders in their efforts to suppress the non-Christians in the Middle East. Whether some historical accounts are apocryphal or true, those who didn't drown in foundering ships, on reaching their destination either died of disease or some other cause or were sold into slavery. Regrettably there has been no better outcome for our own children.

No one was surprised when Wayne La Pierre opened his capacious war chest, leading his NRA and its supporters in a predictable and inevitable counteroffensive propaganda campaign. Presented in the forefront of the opposition to those courageous Parkland students and their followers were La Pierre's own young acolytes. Young people who, either having been brainwashed, bribed, or both, mouthed those cliché phrases we have heard *ad nauseam* about the sanctity of the Second Amendment, and those tired, empty, and fallacious pronouncements such as "It isn't the guns, it's the people who use them," and "The best defense against a bad person with a gun is a good person with a gun." Fallacious because what these cretins are telling us is that we shouldn't get rid of the very objects that are causing the bloody havoc; we should have more of them. And identifying a "good" person from a bad one in our society is becoming as increasingly difficult as it is to distinguish the difference between a Republican and a Democrat.

Clearly this virtually psychopathic obsession with the private ownership of firearms that grips only a *minority* of the population, is driven by the NRA and the gun manufacturers and abetted by the avaricious and cowardly members of *all three branches of our government.* If only that majority Madison feared would deny the minority certain rights and exercise their power this once in a worthy cause. All that is needed is a rephrasing of that pestilential, outdated Second Amendment to the Constitution, and in order to accomplish that we should vote out of office those sycophants who so blithely and idly merely watch while our children and other innocent people are gunned down. But I have begun to think that the only people in the United States who honestly and seriously are concerned about this infamous and increasing violence are the survivors and close friends of the fatalities themselves. Would that the thousands of those guiltless victims now needlessly lost to us could rise up and be heard.

As of 24 March 2018 there already were twenty-two incidents involving firearms discharged on school grounds throughout the country. Of these, eight were intentional attacks during school hours. Due largely to these appalling statistics, a "solution" has been suggested, mainly under the auspices of the NRA and its supporters. Serious lobbying is now underway to permit teachers to carry concealed firearms. After twenty years of intimate involvement with weapons of all kinds and in a variety of settings, some relatively peaceful and others anything but that, I predict that if permission is enacted as law for this doubtful practice at the state, or even worse, at the federal level, it is likely that the armed teacher will be the prime target of the assailant. A practiced shooter will always go for the greatest threat first, whether on the battlefield or elsewhere. And if that teacher's weapon *is concealed* he'd better be as trained and handy as "Quick Draw McGraw" and shoot like "Dead Eye Dick", to cite just two American idols. Currently ten states permit staff members to have guns at their schools.

The NRA, with a membership of over a million and a staff of 300, has the most powerful lobby in Washington and once boasted that it can flood Congress with 500,000 pieces of mail (probably twice that now through use of the internet) virtually overnight in opposition to *any* gun control proposals. This stupid and irresponsible posturing is responsible for much of the confusion that exists over the intent and interpretation of the constitutional right of the individual to bear arms. With hackneyed metaphor the Association warns that infringement is "just the tip of the iceberg" and will, like "the camel's nose in the tent," lead to ultimate withdrawal of the right in its entirety. Their "party line" insists that rather than banning firearms we must apprehend the criminals and somehow screen out those who are psychopathic, sociopathic, or otherwise so mentally impaired as to be incompetent and dangerous, who use firearms for illegal purposes. What a fantastic and forlorn hope made in the teeth of all the evidence proving our abysmal failure to do just that! Truly this is The Devil's Theory brought to life: Political or social crises arise from the deliberate actions of evil or misguided leaders rather than as a natural result of conditions.

In its arrogance and self-assurance of its power the NRA has made no secret that in matters concerning gun control it rates all members of Congress as they would students, from A to F. On a sliding scale those who support NRA policies unequivocally and unquestioningly receive an "A," and those especially zealous and loyal even an "A+", and so on down to a "C." These also receive millions of dollars in donations during election campaigns, again according to the degree of their support for NRA policies. To give you an idea of mean amounts, the NRA donated thirty million dollars to Trump's presidential campaign, while the late John McCain, probably a "B," received as much as seven million. Those graded "D" and "F" are punished at the polls where La Pierre and his disciples do what it takes to see that the failed "student" is voted out of office. This is a form of extortion much like that of Grover Norquist, another powerful political insider and *éminence grise* exerting his influence behind the scenes in the Republican Party. Republican Senators who won't sign Norquist's "pledge" never to support tax increases won't get re-elected.

In my salad days a festive phrase, along with the cheerful and innocent TGIF, was BYOB, bring your own bottle. Today that seems to have been altered to BYOG, bring your own gun. Some wag even suggested recently that the solution to all this school shooting was not to arm teachers, but to hand each child a loaded pistol as he or she entered the school bus.* While we continue to argue, endlessly and in vain, about ways to protect our children from being shot dead while attending school, a single lightning bolt eight miles from the stadium caused a two-hour delay in a first-season football game between Tennessee-West Virginia. In America it's safety first, always. Well, almost always, at least

---

* We can put that suggestion next to the one about making Israel the 51st State.

in most important matters. When I played high school football we kept playing even if the sky was falling. But then, there was very little gun violence in public places except in movies houses, and that was on the screen.

The answer to this continuing, *legitimized,* insane murder spree and the government's indifference and reluctance to admit its true cause has only one answer, and for those who see the problem clearly it is simply this. The selective elimination of the vast majority of individually owned firearms would be the only proof-positive way to stop this devil's round of purposeless killing and wounding (the long-term effect of certain wounds can make the victim wish he hadn't survived). No guns, no shootings. No shootings, no killings. Q.E.D. The first step would have to be to rescind and rewrite that icon of the NRA, the Second Amendment. Alternatively, legislation should be passed to rephrase its controversial and outdated wording so that the states can continue to maintain their legitimate and official *armed forces*. Private ownership would be allowed by application, and if approved after strict background checks, adherence to very strict rules and other basic and sensible conditions must be complied with and backed by severe penalties.

Clearly if something along these lines is not done and done soon this madness will never end; it will only worsen. To envision that those right-minded people who see this simple logic, assuming that there are enough of them, might someday rise up in their frustration and rage and take matters into their own hands is to expect too much. For one thing, many of these people, judging from their very opinions and dispositions, will have no guns. That is not to say that there are those who have guns but sympathize with the first group. But I think that mainly they could not be stirred sufficiently to take any actual action. However, there might be a more agreeable and still effective way to start the effort moving; it would apply the same tactics used by La Pierre's NRA, with an opposite and much worthier objective. If the candidates for legislative office, especially those in the Senate, mainly Republicans but not to the exclusion of their Democrat sympathizers, were assured that if they did not support the great turnabout on gun legislation they would be voted out of office. Vote *in* anyone who failed the NRA test; vote *out* anyone with a passing grade. By standing the NRA's ploy on its head, there might be a chance.

As Winston Churchill once said: "You can always depend on Americans to do the right thing; after they've tried everything else." In connection with such a Herculean effort in a good cause, a crucial factor becomes our electoral system which, much like our infrastructure, is in sore need of repair; it would not be going too far to say it is in need of a complete overhaul. To address that subject is not within the scope of this essay; it will require an additional essay to accomplish that. I can however recommend a source which would be of great help in explaining our present system and its flaws: *Government by the People* by Burns, Peltason and Cronin (2003).

The possibility of strict gun control may offer little promise because a tremendous amount of apathy and inertia would have to be overcome, and that is to say nothing about the lengths to which that rogues' gallery in Washington and their cronies in the NRA and the arms industry would go to maintain the status quo. Of course the bad news is the fact that many Americans, undoubtedly mainly among those who haven't (yet) been scourged by the rampant misuse of firearms, still are just generally apathetic. And we can add to this the fact that the production and sale of firearms is an extremely lucrative business, thus giving us a sinister symbioses: NRA, government, firearms manufacturers and their outlets, not least those mass gun swaps and sales. Still, something must be done, somehow, someday, before the government sees itself losing all control, forcing the country to become a garrison state.

Individual ownership of automatic weapons was banned in this country in 1934, in large part because of the havoc wrought by the use of "Tommy" guns by bootleggers during prohibition. For roughly similar reasons all semiautomatic firearms, which, as I have pointed out, by removal of a little item called a sear can be converted to fully automatic operation, should be banned completely. While the victims during prohibition were mainly underworld figures shot during gang wars, today virtually anyone in this country is susceptible to being gunshot under any circumstances, however innocent (such as a child going to school). As to the camel's nose argument, if banning machine guns in 1934 didn't infringe on the rights of shooters—honest ones—and didn't lead to total banning, why should this?

But will banning just semiautomatic weapons resolve the problem? I think not. We should ban *all* firearms, except obviously those necessary to law enforcement and the armed forces, for at least as long as it takes this runaway society of ours to come back to its senses; then we should make very careful, and very few, exceptions. Anyone who has an interest in hunting and has spent some time in Germany, as only one example, knows what the requisites are for obtaining merely a hunting license and the concomitant right to own a firearm there: intelligence equal to passing the demanding and very comprehensive written and oral examinations, and a civic record which borders on qualification for sainthood. In Italy, which is fraught with organized crime problems almost to the extent that we are, the penalty for illegal possession of a firearm is *eight years imprisonment*, and *three years* merely for possession of illegal ammunition. And when I used to visit Great Britain it was a pure pleasure to be able to approach an unarmed policeman in order to seek his or her assistance or advice. Unfortunately, because of the existing wave of "terrorism" that pleasure would be denied me now. Speaking of illegal ammunition, why should we not invoke, as law, the late Senator Daniel Patrick Moynahan's suggestion, made many years ago? He realized that even if we banned all firearms in the civilian populace, it would be impossible to confiscate all those guns (the number of which now exceed the entire population of the U.S.). Therefore, reasoned Moynahan, we could outlaw the production and distribution of the ammunition required by those firearms. Thus the miscreants, assuming they had the courage, could use their now impotent firearms to club people to death, or perhaps bayonets would come into vogue.

The way matters stand today in American society it should be a privilege, not a right, to own a gun. If someone, using the exception rule, obtains a firearm and then abuses the privilege the penalty should be so severe as to serve as a deterrent to others; this has been shown to work very effectively in other "highly developed" countries. We must face the fact that most firearms today are designed and produced not for hunting or target shooting, but to make it easier to kill people. They're more efficient than knives, clubs, or other, cruder, means. If a person really wants to kill someone we should make it as difficult as possible for him (or her) to do so, not easier.

Additionally, if guns became illegal many of those television and movie characters we now see as heroes— running amok, emptying magazine after magazine of ammunition into their fellow citizens (who too often are inculpable)—would be outlaws. When certain policemen find themselves in a tense, uncertain or dangerous situation, they resort reflexively to foul and repetitive language. This is a sign of fear and anxiety, and consequently the policeman becomes more dangerous than the suspect he confronts. But in such a case the confrontation too often is short-lived. If the suspect, unarmed or not, flees, the policeman, so panicky with fear (and possibly animus or other emotions), may empty his full magazine of ammunition into the other's back.

Possibly because so many policemen in America today are overweight and out of condition, though they may be willing to pursue, capture, and subdue their quarry using equal force, instead they just shoot him down. Subsequent "investigations" into these incidents usually result in a favorable decision for the police officers involved, with no further prosecution or a mild penalty for what in most cases is nothing less than outright, unequivocal murder.* Police at all levels in the U.S. can be much as they are portrayed on TV and in movies—rude, crude in language, bullying, even threatening, regardless of the age or gender of those civilians they encounter. Is it surprising that many of the people in these encounters respond in kind? Perhaps if the police were more respectful in their dealings with reasonable people those people would be more cooperative. What I find ironically humorous, almost bizarre, is that in almost every encounter between a police official and a suspect, or even a culprit caught in the act, the strange deference the officer of the law displays, in seeming to ask permission for his actions. We hear him (or her) say: "We're taking you in, okay?" or "You're under arrest, all right?" Brute force combined with hesitant timidity?

---

* There have been seventy-two Afro-Americans shot dead by policemen in the last two years. In Sacramento, one of the victims, twenty-three year-old Stephan Clark, was shot eight times, six times in the back. He was "armed" with a harmless cell phone. More recently, in Kenosha, Wisconsin, another was shot in the back seven times at point blank range in the presence of his three young children.

What is to be done? In fairness I must concede that the majority of policemen at all levels in this country are not fat, back shooting cowards. Unfortunately it is the rogue officers who usually make the news. There are too few reports of the honest and just majority because these are of less interest than the criminal actions of the latter (if it bleeds it leads).* Bullies almost by definition are cowards. Though in different circumstances a similar mentality and expression of cowardice would apply in the case of a soldier taking an unarmed prisoner to the rear for interrogation and eventual confinement to a POW cage, who shoots the defenseless man, pushes him into a ditch, and returns to his unit.

Sixty years ago a fellow army officer who had been as he described it, "a young beat cop in Harlem in the 1930s," before he enlisted during the war, explained how certain policemen could subdue and arrest a fleeing culprit without giving chase or drawing his pistol. In those days they carried a "nightstick" as well as the standard issue sidearm, a .38 caliber Police Special which holds six rounds. If the fugitive were still ten or less yards away the officer could throw his nightstick, skipping it along the pavement with such skill and accuracy that the runner would trip over it and go down. The officer then would go over, handcuff and arrest his prey, retrieve his stick, call from a nearby call box for a patrol car to take the offender away, and go on with his duties. That officer was Frank Kelly, who ten years after he related this to me and as a full colonel in Vietnam, became the Commanding Officer of the 5th U.S. Army Special

---

* If there is no carnage of any note, unless we lose a serviceman somewhere overseas or we're on the brink of war, domestic news gets priority.

Forces Group. I'd seen that nightstick trick done in an old movie, and an old movie is only that, but having known Frank Kelly I tend to believe it could be done.

Just eliminating all those scenes of gratuitous violence on TV and in films would be a step in the right direction in stemming our seemingly insane drift toward more and more violence. But what should be shown on network and cable television from time to time, as a public service, are some films that reveal what gunshot wounds really are all about. I am certain there are doctors and law enforcement officers all over the country who would be only too eager to participate in such programs.

It is more than ironic that we as a society seem virtually obsessed with safety concerning matters relatively less important than those being discussed. Children's car seats, safe driving rules, bans on smoking, and even Pater Noster elevators and the like take precedence, while we are so seemingly indifferent to more serious matters such as the proven prevalence of chronic traumatic encephalopathy (CTE) among football players in the NFL, and the much more vital issue of gun violence run wild. In the foreseeable future when a TV commercial offers the prudential advice: "Don't leave home without it," they may be referring to a flak jacket rather than a credit card. Mainly, and in short, why don't we just grow up, face this dilemma we have gotten ourselves into and as its framers undoubtedly would be sensible enough to do if they were here now, change the Constitution? We must change that Second Amendment to benefit the great majority of American citizens, not maintain the status quo just for the sake of an archaic tradition or just to please a few wrongheaded citizens, on both sides of the law.

In speaking of the law, it is becoming apparent that this American obsession doesn't bring death, misery and fear merely from the expected quarters. S.W.A.T. (Special Weapons Assault Teams), conceived in the 1960s, were organized, equipped, and trained to meet certain situations such as terrorist attacks or hostage crises that required more than routine force as part of law enforcement. Organized along military lines and armed and equipped with surplus or government donated weapons and vehicles, they now have become a true and formidable paramilitary force. What is alarming is that whereas in the first few decades of their existence they responded to ten or twenty serious situations per year, now their responses are in the hundreds, most in cases where the problem could have been resolved by routine police action or even by one or two regular patrol officers. In their responses to petty criminal situations their actions have been full of flaws in their deployment, supervision, and execution, and thus they have become a virtual scourge in many civilian neighborhoods.

One veteran law enforcement officer described to me their current activities with this analogy: "It's like they're driving in a carpet tack with a ten-pound sledgehammer." Then he added this: "They destroy a lot of private property, too; break down doors, bust windows, tear up lawns with those G.I. armored cars. Even if they don't kill some poor innocent bastard who gets in their way, they scare everybody spitless. And too many times they've even got the wrong effing house!" Though the following anecdote may seem to verge on the fanciful, it is based upon an actual incident involving a S.W.A.T. operation.

Having received a call requesting their assistance in a situation involving illegal drugs, these body-armored and steel-helmeted "warriors," loaded with automatic small arms, thousands of rounds of ammunition, concussion or "stun" grenades, gas masks, battering rams, and other exotic items,[*] went pelting off like one of those "flying squads" of olden times in their MRAP (Mine Resistant Ambush Protected) armored car and other vehicles to the address given.

After breaking in a couple of windows, battering down the door and entering the private residence (probable cause would be their excuse) they found a terror-stricken, elderly woman sitting in a rocking chair. It was revealed later that she was darning her grandson's socks, in the absence of his mother, who had died of a drug overdose. His father was in prison for committing some felony. The boy was at school. After discovering two marijuana cigarettes in the young man's bedroom, the woman was arrested, handcuffed, and taken away to be booked on a drug possession charge. So much for "Hondo" and his merry band of self-styled, heroic commandos. S.W.A.T. teams—paramilitary flying squads full of sound and fury, or as a down-home, rhyme-loving one-time neighbor of mine described them, "A lotta boys full of toys an' noise." The government could at least be honest enough to announce to the populace that they might as well get used to this domestic terror, life at the O.K Corral, saying something like, "This is *America*. Guns are

---

[*] Exotic, yes, and extremely expensive, but the sensible question presents itself: how necessary *is* that overabundance of very costly, top of the line, state of the art equipment? Is it necessary at all? It wouldn't surprise me to learn that some of those pistol magazines were loaded with wad cutters, hollow points, or even those illicit black talon rounds, when standard ball ammunition would be adequate, especially against unarmed civilians.

here to stay; and it isn't the guns that are doing the killing, it's the people using them (police included?). So stop all that whining about your kids being blown away and get on with your lives (unless you're caught in the crossfire)." More band aids on skin cancer.

The violence we are seeing in a number of cities throughout the nation which President Trump ascribes to left-wing "anarchists" who are protesting the growing number of Afro-Americans killed by police under doubtful circumstances can be attributed to the President himself. Aside from tacitly abetting the deaths of what may be a quarter million innocent victims of the COVID-19 virus, by the time you read this (Trump's hobbled postal service permitting), his inciting his followers to violence in those cities will only add to the carnage his self-seeking bungling already has produced. Compared to the deaths for which he is responsible those that were due to police brutality become very small beer indeed. As Adam Schiff, Chairman of the House Judiciary Committee said recently, "Trump is merely fanning the flames of this violence in the streets of our cities." Added to his disgraceful behavior is the probability that should any of his malefactors be charged or indicted for killing any honest and peaceful protesters and should they be convicted and sentenced by their local judicial system (which has been relatively rare), Trump can be expected to grant them a presidential pardon. In Open Letter III, I suggested that Donald Trump makes Mad King George III, against whose reign we rebelled two and one half centuries ago, look like the soul of sanity, rectitude, and serenity. Today, John Dean, former legal counsel to "Tricky Dick"

Nixon, is saying that compared to Trump his former boss of Watergate fame (or infamy) looks like a choir boy.

Now Trump is going to Kenosha, Wisconsin, not to mourn the deaths of Jacob Blake and others during the unrest there, but undoubtedly to drum up electoral support among his base followers in that "battleground" state. While there he will not meet with the Blake family, whose son was shot seven times in the back at point blank range by one of Kenosha's white policemen, and who will be paralyzed for the rest of his life. Although local officials, to include Kenosha's mayor and police chief, with the concurrence of Wisconsin's governor, have told Trump that his presence would only make matters there worse, the President insists on going. I can only add to this what I also said in that same Open Letter III.

> In these dire circumstances, if removing him from office under the provisions of the 25th Amendment failed, truly poetic justice would be served if Trump contracted the virus and died of it. Barring that and in the extreme, the only way of ridding ourselves of this excrescence—one of Nature's worst blunders— would be by assassination. And it seems to me that in such a case the ends of true justice would also be served if the perpetrator(s) were apprehended and tried, the jury would bring in a verdict of not guilty on the grounds of justifiable homicide.

Justice in the United States has been kidnapped and is being held hostage by our legal system. A *speedy* and public trial, as provided by the First Amendment? With two and one half million people already incarcerated there exists a veritable logjam of cases. The court calendars move with glacial speed, not merely because there are so many indictments, but because of the many motions brought forward and not least because of what has become almost *de rigueur* and, in my view, derisive in the system: plea bargaining.

If finally convicted and sentenced to death in those states where certain capital crimes carry that penalty, some of the malefactors die of old age before their scheduled executions. While waiting to be executed, in some cases for *ten or fifteen years,* they have access to legal publications to help them and their court appointed (free) defense attorneys to file their endless appeals. An eighty-one year-old man named Moody, convicted of murder in 1989 and sentenced to death, recently was executed after almost thirty years on death row. Some of those condemned to death write and publish books, while others acquire degrees, in law perhaps, to help them further their efforts to have their convictions overturned. Meanwhile the general populations of convicts enjoy amenities such as weight rooms, TV, library privileges, and rampant homosexuality.* And this is to say nothing of the "recreational" drugs that are routinely smuggled in for their enjoyment.

As to sentencing itself we arrive in the realm of the ridiculous. One hundred young women, at least one of whom was a gold medalist at Rio De Janeiro, have claimed that when they were between the ages of twelve to fourteen they were sexually molested and violated by a Dr. Nassar who was responsible for their medical care during their training at both the U.S.A. Gymnastics organization and Michigan State University. Dr. Nassar was convicted and received *175 years*. We have such absurd decrees as *several consecutive life sentences*. Isn't one life enough? Are the judicial authorities concerned that there might be the possibility of some sort of reincarnation? Somewhat like being convicted *in absentia,* this nonsense is merely symbolic; punishment by verbal condemnation.

Power of course is the handmaiden of wealth, and this combination very often enhances the concupiscent appetite for sex, of some sort, following self-preservation as the second strongest biological urge in humankind. The combination of wealth and the abuse of that source of power undoubtedly makes the path to sexual congress and the fulfillment of one's desires much easier. Currently we are witnessing a virtual avalanche of accusations being made by

---

* The paradox here lies in the fact that while the LGBT community has achieved legal status, and has found approval among many in the general populace, the practice of forcing sex upon unwilling and defenseless convicts (mainly those young and relatively attractive) by older, hard-bitten inmates, often members of gangs, is nothing less than felony rape, in both senses.

alleged victims, mainly female, against men in positions of authority. True consensual sex involves no abuse of authority. Kevin Spacey has been accused of sexually molesting an eighteen-year-old young man on Nantucket Island; Roy Moore, a self-styled Evangelical (or is it Evangenital) former Chief Justice of Alabama's State Supreme Court and now a failed Republican Senatorial aspirant, reportedly molested several young girls, the youngest just fourteen years of age, when he was in his thirties. Harvey Weinstein, the prime target of these accusations of sexual harassment, now has been accused of hiring a company named K2 to assist in suppressing charges made by his alleged victims. Weinstein surrendered to authorities and was released on one million dollars bail. And then there is Jeffrey Epstein, a personal friend of Trump's, and Epstein's personal friend Prince Andrew of the Royal House of Windsor involved in another sex scandal. Epstein's subsequent alleged suicide while imprisoned, awaiting trial, never has been investigated adequately. To paraphrase (liberally) what the late Vince Lombardi is alleged to have said, money isn't everything— it's the *only* thing, to the people who have it. The list of sexual predators is growing exponentially—newscasters, entertainment and other celebrities, members of Congress— daily the names are announced, all holding relatively lofty positions in society. Sexual dalliance seems to plague the office of Attorney General in New York State. Several years ago Elliot Spitzer made his debut, assisted by that trollop from New Jersey, as his wife stood by gritting her teeth. Then Eric Schneiderman was forced to resign in May 2018 over allegations that he had physically beaten not less than four women in pursuit of his sexual gratifications. These are people who were chosen to be the supreme law enforcers in the State of New York, exemplars for all law-abiding citizens.

Now when one sees on TV those Me Too women who hold relatively lofty positions in society, one wonders what attention would be paid to those women in less eminent circles who undoubtedly also have suffered these injustices and indignities. There may be some justice for those of a higher class in our purportedly classless society, certainly for the rich and famous, but that hostage justice I've spoken of does not seem to reach the poor and insignificant, much less the dirt-poor and obscure.* Undoubtedly many are in no financial position to lose their jobs as a result of their complaints or to defray the costs of legal proceedings against the transgressors were they to "come out."

The matter of arbitration is an important factor in these cases of sexual harassment in the work place. Sixty million people in the United States today are in the process of arbitration, not least those involved in cases of sexual harassment or molestation in the work place. That is, those who can afford it. In many cases today job contracts include an arbitration clause. Using the clogged court calendars in civil suits as a reason (or an excuse), the system of arbitration is agreed to by employees who must pay the arbitrators as much as $1000 an hour for their services. Arbitration takes place if not secretly then at least without the publicity that often attends court proceedings, especially those involving celebrities. However, in cases involving sexual harassment or molestation, revelation of that arbitration clause can be

---

* I recognize four classes in our society: the rich and famous; the rich and infamous; the borderline poor and insignificant (to include most of the *intelligencia* and *conociente*); and the dirt-poor downtrodden.

used to help publicize the defendant's complaint. But then, in more contracts than not, especially those drawn up for important and concomitantly lucrative positions, there is a nondisclosure clause, denying the plaintiff the right of revealing any details of the case, not least any names. This is analogous to that ninety-day cooling off period, now thirty days, provided for allegations made by Congressional staffers or even by female representatives. Even Tucker Carlson of Fox News, a defendant himself in a sexual harassment case, admitted that because of arbitration costs, poorer women can't contest the non-disclosure agreements they signed, let alone hire a decent attorney.

And then, ironically, perhaps paradoxically or merely facetiously, the question arises: How do we reconcile public condemnation of these rampant sexual practices while adhering to our convictions about, and commitments to the Anything goes, and I'm okay-you're okay craze sweeping the nation? There certainly seems to be a paradox here. One thinks of such old homilies as What is sauce for the goose is sauce for the gander, and, You can't have your cake and eat it too, and so on. I picture the two Titans of Feminism and Permissiveness in mortal combat. How do we reconcile all this libertine behavior with the feminist strictures on sexual harassment of any kind? The issue comes down to the not so simple matter of intent: consent or denial, and that is where the law steps in to referee, as in cases of statutory rape or child molestation.

As flawed and cumbersome as it has become, we still have *some* system of jurisprudence. So in the matter of sexual harassment (and it is *har*-assment, much as we might like to call it har-*ass*-ment) it comes down to intent and consent or denial. As the pro-abortionists say, a woman has a right to choose. And then there is money, sometimes a good deal of money, as in Trump's lawyer Michael Cohen paying Stormy Daniels for her silence, or a court awarding a plaintiff a large settlement if she proves she was sexually molested or harassed. Some people live in the best parts of two worlds.

To be fair one must admit that to some extent the woman of today may be contributing to this problem, however blameless her intentions. Modern styles in female apparel and their display of a woman's physical charms do little to diminish the concupiscent appetites of normal, healthy men. Unfairly or not the byword must be: "Look, but don't touch," as in a room full of priceless antiques. A blatant example is the sitcom *Two Broke Girls* whose "people pleaser" uniforms barely cover the midsection, or as someone once said, "If their skirts were any shorter they could have worn them for a hat." Excluding those of prurient interest, magazines, not least *Sports Illustrated,* also should be included. In the latter case a buxom Karen McDougal, another of the alleged "Me too" victims (in her allegations involving President Trump), is pictured nude. Are such portrayals an occasion of sin for men, to use an old ecclesiastical expression? And incidentally, that investigation into the allegations made by the porn queen Stormy Daniels against the President and his lawyer Michael Cohen and the continued denials by Trump, continues apace.

Following his farcical meeting with Russia's President Putin at Helsinki in mid-summer 2018, the FBI revealed more information about the President in their earlier search in Trump Tower. They discovered evidence that Roy Cohen, Trump's erstwhile lawyer, who had already admitted he'd paid off porn star Stormy Daniels for her silence, gave Karen McDougal the same amount for the same reason. McDougal alleges that she had a year-long sexual relationship with Trump in the early days of the 2016 presidential campaign.

In mid-August 2018 Trump fired special advisor on racial and other matters, Omirosa Monigault Newman. Newman, better known just as Omirosa, who had appeared on Trump's TV program *The Apprentice* fifteen years earlier, published her highly critical book, *Unhinged*, about Trump and his White House staff. Earlier, she was made (she at first refused) to sign a non-disclosure agreement (NDA). NDAs are common among corporate employees, but relatively new among public service employees. Government employees must sign nondisclosure agreements if dealing with classified information concerning national security, but not those dealing with private matters. Omirosa probably will have a difficult time producing any significant effect with allegations.

Nor is considered the fact that since in general the average woman is not so strong as her male counterpart (despite how she has come to be portrayed on TV and in the movies) she, however unwittingly or unintentionally, is trading upon her physical weakness. In the case of male victims, should they exist, all I could suggest is that they not bring charges, or spend more time at the gym, or both. We should realize of course that all this interaction between the sexes is complicated by a growing impulse toward a transference of gender rôles, with women wanting to be like men and the converse, with men in their growing sentimentality inclining to be women.

Using the same fraternity party scenario, one may ask: why do these young women, some few of them (now becoming so rare as to be on the point of extinction) still *virgo intacta*[*] voluntarily place themselves in such a situation, often knowing beforehand that the house to which they are

---

[*] Recalling my high school days in the 1940s, when there were totally different views on sexual congress, there were two or three girls who were commonly but quietly acknowledged to be of ill repute. In short, they "did it." So with a female population of some 200 in the school, to me, living at the foot of the cross in the Catholic Church and still almost totally inexperienced in these matters, this seemed about right and reasonable. In my relative innocence I assumed that the remaining females led properly chaste lives. But later, though still with no formal training in logic, with all the bragging about sexual trysts that I kept hearing from so many of the boys, in the locker room and elsewhere, it began to seem unreasonable to me that there could be only a couple of girls providing all the fun. For one thing they would hardly have had the time for it. Finally the unarguable truth came home to me. I was no wallflower, and went out on dates with many girls during those days, but somehow I left that school still wearing Cyrano's white plume, a little blemished perhaps, but still intact. I left not feeling any pride or prudish self-satisfaction in myself for having abstained, but rather disillusioned, and more than a little cynical.

bound is reputed to be a hell-hole of debauchery. Too often they go for that very reason: they want to experiment with the forbidden fruit. Some, perhaps those not as attractive by modern standards (mainly physical) and unable to enjoy the popularity they desire, go hoping to achieve popularity, acceptance somehow, even at the cost of being merely exploited, but dispelling any conviction of that end through alcohol or drugs, or both. Others attend merely due to peer pressure, something all second and third raters have experienced since schools were first invented, seeking approval from those they admire and attempt to pattern themselves after. That old saw comes to mind: "So help me, I'll *rape* you!" and the animated and enthusiastic rejoinder, "So rape me, I'll *help* you!"

As to the accused and the actual perpetrators I could say facetiously but perhaps much too conveniently, Well, boys *will* be boys! It's all a matter of temptation, the temptress and the concupiscent appetite; and then there is all this salacious pornography, made too readily available by our modern electronic communications systems. And yes, there is a lack of parental guidance, and all that "I'm okay, you're okay," and "Anything goes" nonsense.

I am not thoroughly grounded in civil criminal law, but I do have a good working knowledge of military and naval justice. Unless there has been a recent change in the Manual for Courts-Martial this "piling on" is akin to the unreasonable multiplication of charges against an individual, called colloquially "stacking charges." As just one example of this illicit practice, a person cannot be charged with both disorderly conduct and assault if the disorderly conduct consisted in making the assault.

Penitentiaries now are "correctional facilities", where order is maintained by corrections officers, not wardens or guards or in the vernacular, "screws," as the "inmates," once convicts, called them. Similarly, insane asylums, booby hatches, or funny farms now are rest homes or sanitariums. Is there any difference in the conditions or environments of these inmates or custodians of these institutions? Or is this simply a case of a rose by any other name, etc.? Whatever else it may be, it certainly is another way those adherents of PC, using euphemisms, further their agenda.*

And then there are those four and one half million people in the U.S. who are on parole or probation (mostly for drug violations), and a number under house arrest, at a cost to the taxpayer of $66,000 per capita per annum. When their time is up, most go back to their old habits.

At the other end of the social spectrum we now have RAGA (Republican Attorneys General Association). RAGA members are State Attorneys General, staunch Republicans, who meet periodically at lavish resorts at no expense to themselves. They are induced to show prosecutorial favor to other Republicans who may be indicted for criminal acts and misdemeanors, in large part white-collar crimes. RAGA raised twenty million dollars in "donations" in its first year of existence. The Democrats, though with less money at their disposal and thus less influence, have a similar counterpart organization. In former more straightforward days and more honest language this was called graft, for that is just what it is.

---

* As to fruitless edicts and matters military, when I was in Bavaria with the U.S. occupation forces after that second war to end wars, an order came down from higher headquarters that "there will be no frostbite." This, when the men riding in steel-decked trucks during a sub-zero winter wearing inadequate standard combat boots before cold-resistant shoepacs were issued, had its ill effect. (A helpful farmer once sold me a couple of bales of straw or hay to strew on the truck beds.) There was no more frostbite reported, but there were a lot of men reporting for sick call with blisters, trench foot, and other poditic disorders. As bad during those days of non-fraternization (or sorasization, to coin a word) was the ban on venereal disease. Many cases of colds and flu were reported as a result of that one until the medics made higher headquarters visit reality.

Another judicial injustice recently has been revealed. In South Carolina a woman was sentenced to twenty-one days in jail because she did not have the $2000 needed to pay a traffic violation, and other states have begun to follow suit. Traffic fines have become so exorbitant as to make it impossible for poorer people to pay them. Of course the reason they are so high is that so many of the states, counties, and municipalities in the United States do not have sufficient funds to meet their expenses. If the governments, following the outrageous example at the federal level, at every level, can't meet their fiscal responsibilities the burden falls upon the people. In short, with so much wealth held at the top in this winner take all society, the rest of the people are going bankrupt.

A more insidious problem has been gnawing at justice in this country as well, and rapidly is reaching unmanageable proportions. It is a constitutional right for an accused person to be provided a proper defense at government expense if he is unable to pay for his own attorney. The caseloads of our public defenders have reached a point where an accused person must spend as long as six months, *in jail,* waiting for his court-appointed attorney to get to his case. These public attorneys now are trying to handle three to five times as many cases as they should be expected to. Although I'm sure that most of these beleaguered lawyers are doing their best, it is only too obvious that they are on the horns of a classic dilemma: either they must rush through one case to get to the next, conscious-ridden by the knowledge that they needed more time to prepare their case (examining evidence, discovery, interviewing potential witnesses) and didn't have it; or, they apply due and scrupulous diligence to every case, and let those who are languishing in durance vile wait their turn.

This unjust and disgraceful state of affairs must be addressed and corrected. It's a matter of money, as it is with many other things that need fixing: more (qualified) public defenders and higher salaries for all those "defenders of the common man." The inability of so many to come up with bail means they are remanded to jail to await trial. What about that golden thread that runs through our system of jurisprudence, the presumption of innocence (unlike France)? There should be a "rolling fund" for public defenders to use for bailing out their defendants. When bail is turned in it would go back into the fund and so continue to be used for those poor (in both senses) bastards. The money that would be saved in maintenance of those awaiting trial could be used to defray at least some of the new expenses for hiring and raises in pay.

One of the many potential dangers of PC is to be found in the law courts. A white man murders a black man whom his sister intends to marry. The white man has rigid feelings about intermarriage, he may even dislike or hate blacks. He's indicted on the murder charge, and the prosecutor adds the "surcharge" that this is a hate crime, making sentencing potentially even more severe should the murderer be convicted. But can emotions be legislated? Has it become illegal and punishable for someone to hate another, perhaps an entire race, even if he takes no action other than voicing this opinion (but not publicly as an incitement to riot)? Where would this end? Can love or sorrow under certain circumstances be punishable by law?

In discussing this matter of political correctness as it affects our relationship with Israel, I took the position that however hard its adherents attempt to employ its doubtful doctrines to further their interests, political correctness cannot be legislated. The Canadians, however, or at least their lawmakers, seem to disagree. "The bill C-16," says Jordan Peterson, a Harvard professor from Toronto, "… are the first laws…that require people under the threat of legal punishment to employ certain words, speak in a certain way, instead of merely limiting what they have to say." He goes on to say that "not only would using someone's preferred pronouns be considered discrimination under the new human rights legislation, it would be a form of hate speech…. We [are] in danger of placing certain kinds of language into the same category as Holocaust denial." The House of Commons voted in favor of the bill, sponsored by the Ontario Human Rights Commission, in October 2017. It will go before the Justice Committee next. Ontario is the first Canadian province to consider such legislation. One response from the U.S. to this Canadian controversy came from the LGBT Resource Center at the University of Wisconson-Milwaukee: "{G}ender-neutral and gender-inclusive pronouns are the result of languages, like English, not having a gender-neutral or third-gender pronoun (as in the German *der, das, den*). Nowhere in the U.S. Constitution is the universal singular male pronoun not used."

Finally, there is the matter of the injustices and inequities in court decisions, based upon the status, class, or celebrity of the accused. The O.J. Simpson case has become a juridical joke, much as the Twinkie Defense, or that ham sandwich used as an example of how easy it is to get a Grand Jury

Indictment. Along with all this there are the prisons such as "Club Fed" (as in Club Med) to which such notables as Bernie Madoff, organized crime heads, and high-ranking politicians are sent. As to politicians, as one positive result of the Me Too explosion, members of Congress no longer can benefit from that ninety-day "cooling off period" rule before any action is taken following allegations of sexual harassment or molestation by other Congressional members or staffers.

September 24, 2020

To paraphrase the French philosopher Voltaire, who in describing the British once said: "They have 565 religions, but only one sauce," I would say in describing the "Americans" that they also have at least 565 religions but only one God—Mammon (and in deference to the French palate only one cheese—cheddar, and perhaps some undefined product that goes by the name of Colby). Whatever the state of our society, money, the striving for wealth, in too many cases (see the Forbes 400 listing) wealth merely for its own sake continues unabated. Another Frenchman, Alexis de Tocqueville wrote about this fiscal obsession 180 years ago in his two-volume work *Democracy in America (1835-1840),* based upon his observations while traveling through what then comprised the United States of America. In his own words:

> "I know of no country, indeed, where the love of money has taken stronger hold on the affections of men and where a profounder contempt is expressed for the theory of the permanent equality of property.... The love of wealth is therefore to be traced, as either a

principal or accessory motive, at the bottom of all that the Americans do; this gives to all their passions a sort of family likeness."

Now, due mainly to the virtually insane striving of our President to secure a second term, we are engaged in, and losing, the battle against a horrific viral pandemic which future historians (should there be any left) will refer to as the great COVID-19 disease. We can only hope that a change in leadership will lead to our ultimate survival. But let us pretend for a moment that this horrific unseen enemy had not attacked us; that the shattering blows it has dealt to our economy—resulting in the expenditure of trillions more dollars added to our already astronomical national debt—don't exist. Let us look at our economic structure as it was in more "normal" times. Sometimes a retrospective "look in the mirror" can be helpful in times of crisis such as this is. As dismal as our economic situation is now and however grim it may appear for the future, perhaps this quandary in which we find ourselves may be an opportunity to see more clearly our financial ills (the inequitable distribution of wealth being one of many) and so find the means to cure them.

I think that one of the main factors that drives this almost obsessive lust for money lies in the barrenness of American society: with no aristocracy, no familial celebrity or ancestry, societal philosophy, i.e., no true class system. Money alone is the criterion for esteem within the population. I am always grateful I had no ancestors on that wretched Mayflower, which contained its share of the dregs of English society— criminals, religious fanatics, and worse. Small wonder then, that as De Tocqueville astutely observed, among the former colonists there was this virtually inordinate craving for wealth. These newly liberated people, mainly from the lower classes of English society, little better than those in Australia who had been transported for terms of years or even lifetime exile, under the British class system had been subjugated by "the Gentry," the "Quality," (or put more commonly, "the carriage trade"). It did not take long for the realization, among the more enterprising but perhaps less principled of these people, newly liberated from the strictures of the then mainly ancestrally based class system in England, that wealth itself could become a class distinction within this new and nominally classless country.* Only the Australians, who live in what once was a British penal prison colony, have as bleak a heritage.

---

* An awareness that was to occur more gradually and subtly in England after the Industrial Revolution. And the Southern cotton planters, through their slaves' labor, along with the merchants of the North, were among the first to acquire that wealth (and those carriages). And so this penchant continues, not excluding those who have become rich as Croesus as entertainment or sports celebrities. The rich go on trying to buy their way into heaven, with their foundations, arts patronage, trusts, charities, and epidemiological campaigns in distressed countries, as did their predecessors—the Carnegies, the Rockefellers, the Vanderbilts, and the other robber barons of that Gilded Age of more than a century ago, when Social Darwinism had set in with a vengeance. Today's Limousine Liberals, the rich and famous, go on with lives in the Hamptons, Palm Beach, and Palm Springs, and other plush resorts while the poor and insignificant go on with their mediocre, or worse, existences, hoping for those better times which always seem to be just out of their grasp. As the late Robin Leach used to sign off his popular TV show *Lifestyles of the Rich and Famous,* it's "Champagne wishes, and caviar dreams" for too many Americans. Yes, for some forty million people in the U.S. living beneath the poverty level, that's pretty much all they've got—wishes and dreams. I suggest you read Anand Giridheradas' recently published book, *Winners Take All; The Elite Charade of Changing the World,* for more insight into this masked but very real injustice.

Just look at what's happened to us. A hundred years ago Ford's Model T's were crawling about all over the known world, while Kodak cameras were taking pictures of them wherever they went, and ton upon ton of Carnegie's high-grade steel was being shipped everywhere to build the world's railroads, bridges, and edifices, and yes, its warships and artillery pieces for those merchants of death. Today we just can't compete successfully with other industrial nations, some of which we used to despise and ridicule—look at the ever increasing conflict over tariffs. "Globalization" won't work in our favor as long as producers such as China, Singapore, Korea, Taiwan, or Bangladesh, to name a few, pay low wages in their sweat shops. We can get our way, mainly with money—in both ways: financial aid or sanctions—but when we try to affect their internal financial affairs, not so much, as the current "buzz phrase" has it.

Check that trade deficit again and look at the labels. You don't see "Made in the U.S.A" much anymore because, except for certain electronic products, we manufacture fewer and fewer items here at home. We seem proud to pronounce on a given TV commercial that the product was "assembled in the U.S.A." with no credit given to say, Mexico, where the item was actually manufactured. Otherwise all we're making here at home is taco shells and those pharmaceutical products that, owing to ineptitude, indifference, and avarice, have led to the current disastrous and increasing drug crisis we are experiencing today.

Yes, we've got to compete with cheap labor overseas, but one reason we're falling so far behind is because of what's happened to our educational system. Except for our graduate schools (which increasingly are swarming with foreign students, many of whom stay on and take jobs here), we're ranked *dead last* among the so-called developed countries in educational excellence, especially in math and science. When you hear that unemployment has dropped here in America you can bet it's because more people have been hired at McDonald's or Taco Bell, or somewhere else in the service industry where mainly no great skills are needed, certainly not in math and science. Meanwhile, our factories continue to close and thousands are being laid off, to the great satisfaction of foreign manufacturers throughout the world. A global trade or tariff war, which President Trump still is stubbornly precipitating will only add to our economic and financial imbalances.

As to our imminent financial collapse, I no longer blame merely the Government, Big Business, the Media or the symbiotic collusion among all three that's been obvious for decades or longer. No, I've begun to see that it's the general public, the *people themselves* who are largely to blame—in their apathy, stupidity, and ignorance—who are permitting their own ruin. While the national debt now exceeds *twenty three trillion dollars* they're lining up in the small hours waiting for stores to open on "Black Fridays"—as merely one example—so they can buy "cheap" computers and TV sets with money they should be using to buy food for their children.

The TV relentlessly urges the people to Buy, Buy, BUY! when in good conscience they should be telling them to Save, Save, SAVE! But then they've got you there too. If you're saving your money in a bank and not under your mattress you'll receive the bountiful interest rate of about *one quarter of* one *percent* of your capital! You can thank that central bank in Washington, euphemistically and obscurely named the Federal Reserve, in collusion with Wall Street, which is booming again, and any number of our "representatives" in Congress for that situation. And speaking of the Federal

Reserve, commercial banks, and the SEC (Securities and Exchange Commission), whatever happened to all that money that was stolen in the savings and loan banks? In October 2001 the scandal at ENRON and the company's collapse left hundreds of thousands of people without any hope of a secure retirement through the loss of their 401K savings. A couple of years ago, a docudrama was produced called *Small Enough to Jail,* a play of words on the "Too big to fail," that described those big commercial banks that caused the 2008 recession and which paid only millions in fines while getting billions from the U.S. Treasury to stay afloat. The story centered on Abacus, a small neighborhood bank in Chinatown, New York that was prosecuted for a malfeasance which they were investigating and cleaning up themselves. Abacus Bank was small, relatively powerless in Washington, so they were targeted to show the public the government was doing *something* about all the greater malfeasance and crooked trading.

While over forty million people in the U.S. continue to live in poverty, and more than one third of Americans now have no retirement plan, the top ten percent possess or control ninety percent of its wealth. Much has been said and written about that .01 percent of the U.S population who possess a disproportionate majority of its wealth. Matthew Stewart, in a cover article for the *Atlantic* magazine, concentrated on the next 9.9 percent who command most of the rest. To be qualified for membership in this group one must possess a net wealth of 1.2 million dollars (houses, real estate, cars, boats, etc.). The median net worth among these people is 2.4 million. In the current social climate of rising inequality, while they continue to consolidate their wealth through diversified investments, they live in the best areas of the country (Westchester County, the Hamptons, Shaker Heights, Grosse Point, Palm Beach, etc.) and many of their residences are in gated, and now *gated and guarded* communities. Their children attend private or the top public schools, which are socially (geographically), if not legally, segregated, and they have infinitely better health coverage than the great majority of people.

Reminiscent of the once great noble and royal houses of Europe, they intermarry among their own "class," keeping pace in pursuit of maintaining and increasing their wealth and power, while as a general rule those in the "lower classes" marry within that class, and thereby remain socially and financially static. Upon encountering these upper middle class people, they seem kind, but under the surface they are quietly but unquestionably egoistic. While millions are jobless during the current pandemic and begging aid, scandalously, that .01 percent I spoke of has increased its wealth by 851 billion dollars.

Not least is the more subtle matter of inflation, which the government continues to insist does not present a problem. There can be no comparison with what it was like in post World War I Germany when mothers were pushing wheel barrows full of *bundles of billion mark* notes to the shops to buy a little bread and butter for their children.* Since the Reagan years, with their supply-

---

* Due almost entirely to the vicious and vindictive actions of the Anglo-French in imposing outrageous reparations payments, coupled with the British blockade of German ports, which went on for almost a year after the Armistice in November 1918, and the appropriation of their ships, dirigibles, and whatever else served their purposes, the Germans literally were starving to death. The United States accepted their fair share of the spoils.

side or trickle-down economics, inflation has continued its rise while salaries remain static. All the while we hear platitudinal pronouncements from "informed government sources" telling us that everything continues to improve economically. But if you did have a thousand dollars saved somehow, somewhere, you'd be better off spending it now, perhaps on something like that Black Friday spree, because a year from now that $1000 would only buy about two thirds of what it would today. So now they've got you three ways.

The dismal truth is that the people who can afford to invest in stocks and bonds don't need the money they may profit. As St. Matthew said (13:12) "For whosoever hath, to him shall be given, and he shall have more abundance." The great majority of the people who actually gain from stocks and bonds are those who don't need the money, just as they don't need health insurance because they can afford to pay for virtually *any* medical care they may need. And that old joke about banks only approving loans for people who don't need the money is true also. If you're honest but desperate for money, you'd better have something more tangible than your word, like collateral, or at least a steady and adequate income.

Nationwide, some *three trillion dollars* is being drained steadily from the pension funds of honest employees throughout the nation. Without the financial aid they have been promised I envision a great number of elderly Americans almost literally "dying in their traces" in the foreseeable future. And in the not too distant future, with a budget deficit approaching a trillion dollars and a national debt of over twenty-three trillion, I see something similar happening on the federal level involving such programs as Medicare and the Social Security System.

Always overshadowed by Wall Street, a look at "Main Street" is revealing. Those who have little money and who comprise the vast majority of people in the U.S. today can't invest for fear of losing their little all in the gamble, and playing the market *is* a gamble. Any sensible gambler at cards will tell you never to enter a game unless you have enough money to cover the stakes, and as important, unless you can afford to lose that money. Of course if the market resumes its downward plunge towards the wines and spirits due to this pandemic at least there should be a substantial rise in interest rates as applied toward those little savings accounts.

Then there is the "pension gamble." Throughout the United States firemen, policemen, teachers, and other state employees are in dire threat of losing their promised, lawful retirement pensions, along with assured health care benefits. Thus far Kentucky is in the most serious jeopardy, but other states are sure to follow. This ominous situation, pension gamble, as it has come to be called, has resulted from the inept practice of investing millions, if not billions of dollars, from the pension funds or systems, as some call them, in unstable or risky companies listed on the New York Stock

Exchange. These risky investment transactions have been induced by the shrewd connivance of the Wall Street brokers combined with the innocent ineptitude of those members of the pensions fund committees, many of whom, though they may be adequate or even excellent in the teaching, law enforcement, or other fields which they have chosen, are tyros in financial matters.

The so-called Placement Agents sent out to meet with those who control the states' pension funds are paid large fees (millions in some cases) to induce those mainly honest but ignorant controllers to make investments in doubtful or even fraudulent stock market entities. Among themselves with their astute guile they refer to the funds invested under their advice as "dumb money." Added to this misrepresentation there are hidden fees given to people all along the investment process which milk the retirement funds even more (as in the case of many 401K plans). Now, as the pension systems are being ruthlessly depleted, the state budgets, which still are suffering, some literally reeling, from the recession caused by the outrageous malfeasance of the Wall Street banks in 2008, have had to reach into those very pension funds to satisfy their other budgetary requirements—legitimate requirements, such as for roads and bridges (which are falling into disrepair all over the country) that must be maintained as well as other necessary expenses—which must be met. So while government agencies at all levels in a given state will continue to survive by draining its pension fund, that same fund is being depleted by unsound investments. This is nothing more than a fool's paradise, created by a combination of ineptitude on the part of the pension committees and the tempting but fraudulent "opportunities" presented to them by those avaricious agents from Wall Street. Eventually the state's entire fiscal structure will come down like a house of cards, while most of its retirees, hard-working, innocent and trusting members of its society, will live out their lives in destitution.[*]

All this is reminiscent of that Gilded Age, at the end of the nineteenth and beginning of the twentieth centuries, when such robber barons as J. Pierpont Morgan, Andrew Carnegie, John D. Rockefeller, and Cornelius Vanderbilt, to name a few, were holding the nation's purse strings and its entire financial structure in the palms of their hands. Gilded perhaps, but as one wise observer commented recently in a PBS production focused on that social blot on our historical copybook (one among too many during that notorious age) and I paraphrase: "Gilt isn't gold by any means; it simply is something attractive that masks something unattractive, some baser metal beneath it." During this notorious age and soon after the Great War, when returning veterans found no jobs awaiting them, slogans such as "Rich men wage war; poor men fight them," abounded. Strikes caused by this and the inequities of low wages and excessive working hours for those who did have jobs began to spring up all over the country.

---

[*] Add to this one of President Trump's lying claims: that he will reduce the outrageous cost of drugs (which many of the elderly depend upon to stay alive), forcing many U.S. citizens to go to Canada, where the drugs are much cheaper. The irony lies in the fact that due to our utter failure in controlling COVID-19, the Canadians have closed their border to us. Another "A" to add to Trump's laurels. It doesn't please me to add that the 600,000 American expatriates already residing in Canada are fortunate, in more than one respect, not least in not having to risk their lives due to our gross mismanagement of the great pandemic we are enduring.

Adam Smith, who can be said to have invented the system of modern capitalism, admits that while wealth is the driving force of capitalism it must be accompanied by what he called sympathy, which interpreted in common parlance means consideration for those lower in the financial structure of an economy. There must be an equitable distribution of that wealth as it is achieved, in other words, sharing. The United States, for reasons already stated, would be a difficult place in which to plant such a tender seedling as capitalism, not least to nurture it and see it grow. For that reason, to expect any success merely through good will there must be sanctions. We cannot depend upon (using a hackneyed phrase) Man's Love For His Fellow Man. Laws would have to be enacted, and strictly enforced. This would be aided in vast measure commensurate with those corrupt campaign finance practices I have spoken about.

Recently in a TV presentation dealing with financial inequities, a well-dressed elderly man was pictured on his twenty-five-million-dollar yacht. He was carrying a large silver tray laden with succulent looking slices of beef, obviously on his way to enjoy himself with friends aboard. Later, while gazing out over the expanse of the marina in which his yacht was anchored, and as the camera panned around revealing yachts and sailboats, mainly white and of all sizes, he commented on how this scene was analogous to and represented the various levels of success and concomitant wealth in this, our national structure of free enterprise capitalism. "Most of those boats aren't as large as mine and some are small, but maybe the owners are lucky, because they've got smaller problems." I found myself almost praying that as one of those smaller boats (smaller but also very new and expensive) went by its skipper would call out, "Hey! That big barge must give you a lot of headaches. Wanna trade?"

Possibly to follow capitalism (introduced 500 years ago), fascism, and communism, the latter two inimical of the true idea of capitalism, there may now come what some political economists identify as the Sharing Economy. In Uruguay former President José Mujica introduced "managed companies" wherein all employees have a voice in the management system to include pay scales. There now are forty such commercial units in Uruguay. The president of Gravity Payments, a credit card processing firm in Seattle, whose annual salary was one million dollars has cut his own wage to $70,000 and raised the salaries of *all his employees* to the same amount. In more humble terms residents in the Netherlands have begun practicing a scheme of lending-sharing, with wealthier families assisting their less fortunate neighbors with loans of money and gifts of household items.

Many people began seeing Leninist communism as a possible answer to what they perceived had become a "have and have not society." In May 1919 a large bomb went off opposite the J.P. Morgan Building at Wall and Broad Streets in New York's financial district, killing twenty-nine people and wounding 200 others. Newspaper headlines screamed about "Terror", and "Terrorists." With this "foreigners" began to be rounded up and deported, among them the anarchist Luigi Galleani, who government officials thought was responsible for the Wall Street bombing (never proven). Clearly that nebulous "enemy" Terrorism is not new to the United States. There have been other acts of terrorism, most notably in recent times the homegrown, all-American bombing of that library in Oklahoma City, compliments of that all-American young man, Timothy McVeigh. As George Kennan said, "we must always have an enemy," and if we can identify and cite no other more tangible enemy, Terror must do.*

However, what too many people in America seem to ignore or just fail to grasp is that when this "enemy" comes to act against us, the government, without fail, treats only the symptoms, the results, and ignores the root causes of these horrific acts. *Why* did that bomb go off a hundred years ago? *Why* did those planes crash into the World Trade Towers nineteen years ago?

One-third of Americans now have no retirement savings; they must work just to stay alive, if they can find work, as long as they *can* work. What does *this* say for the "land of opportunity"? In the event of an emergency requiring $400, half the families in this country couldn't come up with enough money to see it through without selling something or doing without something they truly need. Wages continue static with no universal and reasonable minimum wage. Meanwhile organized labor is being stifled at the behest of those Wall Street sponsors' political aspirants. If one factors in those in the work force who have given up trying to find decent jobs and those who do not want to bag groceries or

---

* TV in its sheep-like, profit-seeking way of utilizing current events to provide a sense of current threats, battens on this embedded trend in its myriad series of police and other government agency procedurals. They have substituted the Russian mobsters in "Little Odessa," or their Asian equivalents from Japan (*Yakuza*), China, and other Eastern countries for the now passé Italian Mafia. In place of the Soviet Cold War threat we are given the North Koreans or Iran, or simply Islamic "terrorism." If Putin and the new Russia begin to act with more hostility, those hungry but careless TV producers will find even more fertile fields to sow.

flip burgers in part-time jobs which do not entitle them to any benefits, unemployment presently is closer to eighteen or twenty percent rather than the three or four percent the government is touting.*

When the national debt was approaching a mere trillion dollars twenty or thirty years ago, *Time* or *Newsweek* published an article on the subject, and in a sidebar cited two examples to explain just what a trillion dollars amounted to. One claimed that if one of those ancient Greeks, say Socrates, had been given a trillion dollars and told he could spend it at a million a day, and if he were still alive, he'd still be spending it today! Some simple arithmetic will verify that. But does anyone understand this, or care? Now we no longer can afford to pay, mainly to the Chinese, Japanese, and Saudis, merely the *interest* on the money we've borrowed from them. Meanwhile, with 700 military and naval bases around the world and with our almost routine "small" wars launched without truly legitimate provocation we're still programming almost *one trillion dollars a year* for our "defense"† budget alone. What will it take to wake the people up?—probably nothing short of a nuking of the United States.

---

* And this is to say nothing about the shambles the pandemic has wrought of the workforce and their families.

† Which thanks to our government and our own indifference may possibly be the greatest example of euphemism in the lexicon today.

October 1, 2020

I n the mid-eighteenth century, Sam Johnson started two periodicals, *The Rambler* and *The Idler*, which to some literary critics were heavy, overly didactic imitations of Joseph Addison's earlier periodicals. I consider these open letters to be didactic, and intentionally so. These are serious matters of which I speak, some so serious as to bear upon the very survival of this country as a democracy, however imperfect, so also is the title "Rambler" appropriate to this letter. What follows will be a digressive, but instructive, perhaps even entertaining commentary touching on various parts of the large canvas which constitutes the American sociopolitical landscape. And, as you read, I should remind you that it was the same Johnson who said, "Patriotism is the last refuge of a scoundrel."

Let's start with the forthcoming election. What could be the results? Trump could win by a clear majority, and we would have only ourselves to blame for what we have to endure for the next four years. Trump won in 2016 because our government was even then corrupt, with injustices everywhere, not least our shameful, inequitable distribution of wealth. Trump, setting himself up as a champion to cure our ills, only made matters worse by systematically polarizing the populous with his deceits and a series of true crimes and misdemeanors, euchering his mainly innocent but largely ignorant (with the exception of our graduate schools we have the worst educational system in the world) and gullible followers into seeing him as some sort of martyred savior. So corruption developed apace into an infinitely worse form under his totally inept, self-seeking, and amoral "leadership". Trump may be mad, he may be a semiliterate bully but, as they say in the deep south, He's a wily bird, and he's got more (deceptive) moves than a mama chipmunk. And because the devil is such a busy man, he's been very lucky. Moreover, it's an unfair game Donald Trump is playing, unfair because he is consciousless and totally amoral, while too many of his opponents are decent people; yes, ignorant, even indifferent, but still decent. Why do we, the people, always seem to give him the home field advantage? But let us go back to the election.

The untimely death of Justice Ginsberg gave President Trump an opportunity he quickly seized, and that opportunity has a number of benefits, as Trump would see them. The Republican majority in the Senate, with Majority Leader McConnell leading the charge, will do their utmost to rush through Amy Coney Barrett's confirmation hearings, and though the Democrats will strive mightily to prevent her confirmation before the election on 3 November, and however much Biden pleads with the U.S. public not to abide Barrett's confirmation, they will fail.

With the Court then stacked in Trump's favor a number of his political objectives can be realized. The first of these concerns the election itself. Unless Biden wins in a landslide, to include both the 270 votes required by the Electoral

College as well as the popular vote, all should be serene, otherwise, Trump may contest the outcome, thus delaying the final decision for an untold period of time, and like the Bush-Gore contretemps of the 2000 election, will finally be decided by the Supreme Court. With three Trump selectees and that Republican automaton Clarence Thomas deciding in his favor, and barring an unfavorable vote from Chief Justice Roberts, Trump could claim another resounding victory.

But there is more. Trump and his corporate coconspirators, to include the major banks, and especially those insurance giants in the health management business, have wanted to rid themselves once for all of Obama's Affordable Care Act (ACA). The President has been promising that he has his own plan, which he ensures us will include that provision for preexisting medical conditions such as cancer, diabetes, heart disease and now and not least, medical conditions connected with the COVID-19 virus. When questioned about his promised health plan to replace Obama care, he has said almost without exception that he would announce its details "in a couple of weeks" (or if asked in mid-month, "by the end of this month"). Trump has no such plan, unless in his perverse way he plans to eliminate the existing ACA through a Supreme Court decision, where it is already under adjudication, and again, with his stacked court he may well do it. Trump's case against the ACA will go before the court on 10 November. It would be unnecessarily repetitious to cite other issues to which he would apply the same stratagem; vital matters such as striking down the Roe v. Wade decision; the DACA (Deferred Action for Childhood Arrivals) question and immigration policy in general; police brutality; and freezing gun control laws under the provisions of that dubiously worded Second Amendment to the Constitution.

Trump has made himself perfectly clear about his position on climate change, an even greater threat than the current pandemic, if that can be imagined. Aside from walking out on those Paris climate accords, he has neutered the EPA (Environmental Protection Agency). And how about those fires on the West Coast and those record-setting hurricanes in the Gulf of Mexico? I can hardly say more about the COVID-19 pandemic than you've already read elsewhere in these archives.

Meanwhile, those who only grumble and dither about all this, those who are in a position to do something about our being on the verge of becoming an autocratic, authoritarian nation of sheep, do nothing. We elected this man Trump, to our great cost as it turned out. There is nothing under the laws of this country that decrees a sitting President cannot be impeached more than once; the President himself has handed us the grounds on a plate (the provisions of that 25th Amendment still linger). If Biden wins the election, at least we'll have someone who's sane in the White House; but since I am somewhat cynical by nature, my pessimism impels me to say that even should he win, eventually, human nature being what it is, things will return to the *status quo ante* Trump. Big business with all its inequities and injustices will once again prevail and we will find ourselves in the same socioeconomic conditions that Trump so shrewdly battened upon to get elected. Why do I find myself wondering what Ross Perot would have done if he had become President in 1994?

Despite all this, to include what our future may hold, many of those foreign observers who Trump cordially despises, must be looking at us wonderingly as a goodly part of our semiliterate society is saying, "Don't confuse me with facts; I've made up my mind," while our President is telling the rest of us, "Be reasonable, see it my way."

October 6, 2020

With respect (in both senses) to Sam Johnson, let us continue our ramble through this ill-fated and maladministered garden of socioeconomic politics in America.

Much like the chimera of communism, the system of democratic capitalism we have practiced as a result of the Industrial Revolution is failing rapidly. In both forms of governance this failure has the same root cause, and that lies in the nature of Man himself. In theory, Karl Marx had a good idea, but with an insurmountable flaw: its success or failure depended upon the innate qualities of those who would want to enjoy its fruits. Eventually, those benefits of his theory proved inaccessible because of what Thomas Aquinas spoke of and wrote about nine hundred years ago.

Yes, I am speaking, as was Aquinas so long ago, philosophically, not religiously, of those Seven Deadly Sins to which Man became susceptible at the point when humans evolved from Homo Erectus to Homo Sapiens, viz., when (somehow) we became endowed with an intellect and a free will. Would you find it tiresome if I list them here?—Pride, Envy, Wrath, Sloth, Lust, Avarice (money), and Greed (insatiable appetite for material goods, to include food and drink). If only numerically they always have preempted, not to say overwhelmed those altruistic Four Cardinal Virtues of Prudence, Justice, Temperance, and Fortitude. The odds were too great, mainly because those who were meant to benefit from and enjoy those fruits of such Utopian concepts as Communism or Democracy were denied them by their very frailties. As I've written elsewhere, even poetically: You can't make a good pot out of poor clay. Of interest here is the fact that the ancient Greeks, despite their enlightened intellectualism and political acuity discovered, 2000 or more years ago, that democracy did not work. In more recent times it was Winston Churchill who said, and I paraphrase, Democracy is anything but perfect, but it's better than its alternatives. So perhaps it was not too difficult for Aquinas, living in Sicily a thousand years after those Greeks had occupied it, to draw his conclusions about Man's susceptibilities and vulnerabilities, his flaws and frailties, in a word, his concupiscence, as the species of animal life the anthropologists are pleased to call Homo Sapiens (wise, intelligent man). Better perhaps Homo Homini Lupus (man as a wolf to man) if you keep up with the daily news.

It was with bitter amusement to hear that I, as a retired soldier living on half pay, paid more in federal taxes in 2016 and '17 than our self-proclaimed billionaire president. I derived some consolation, however, in hearing also that he owes debts amounting to almost a half-billion dollars (some very authoritative sources are saying that the amount actually is more than a billion dollars) with payment due during the next two or three years. It is interesting to speculate about what might happen to him if he defaulted when he no longer was president. And to whom does he owe such a vast sum? Someone out there knows "where the bodies are buried," and, if Trump defaults that may be the time to disclose their location(s).

Those debts are owed by Trump personally, but who holds the markers for the twenty-three trillion-dollar national debt? Turkey may be one of the minor lenders; Turkey, for whose benefit Trump abandoned our best allies in Syria, the Kurds. Certainly Saudi Arabia is a major lender and who, in collusion with the fragile Yemenese government continues to murder and starve to death the civil populace that has risen against it; Saudi Arabia, that with Turkish cooperation murdered and then dismembered an American foreign correspondent. And perhaps Russia, that supplied the Assad regime with weapons and provided them military support in putting down the Syrian insurrection. Yes, Russia, that put bounties on the heads of U.S. troops in Afghanistan and is still negotiating with Trump about erecting a Trump Tower in Moscow, and continues to enjoy relatively free reign in their campaign to retake control of the Ukraine without interference by a U.S. distracted and beleaguered by the pandemic. And at this point in our domestic politics what may be most important, the Russians being permitted, and even encouraged by the present administration to engage in disrupting and influencing our domestic politics, and not least our federal elections. Then there is China which along with Japan and Saudi Arabia is one of our major financial "benefactors," but which Trump continues to excoriate over the pandemic. North Korea, though in no position to extend financial aid (and seeing no need to do so) has been virtually ignored in her continuing efforts to achieve her long-standing objective of becoming the preeminent nuclear power in her area of the Far East.

In short, we continue to lose our battles on the domestic front while we are fast losing our status as a global leader. Meanwhile, caught in the throes of this runaway pandemic, the control of which has been bungled since its outset by the very leaders to whom we should look for guidance during such a crisis, we are incapable of dealing with such crucial matters as I have mentioned.

The presidential "debate" in Cleveland on the 29th September was something between bad French farce and The Gong Show. (Could the choice of Cleveland, with its famed medical clinic, have played a part in the uncertainty of the president's testing regimen?) In any case, as if we weren't already the object of the world's somber derision, those "foreigners" must now be laughing at us through their pandemic induced tears of despondency.

October 13, 2020

President Trump's removal from office, whether due to the results of having contracted the COVID-19 virus or, however dilatorily, by losing the election, or, by at last resorting, to the provisions of the Twenty-fifth Amendment will be a welcome but joyless relief. However vindicated some of us would feel there will always linger the haunting specter of those hundreds of thousands of needless deaths he will leave behind. It begins to be probable that our hesitance in attempting to remove this traducer of our own creation, or the poetic justice of his dying from the very efforts of the catastrophe he in great part produced, will leave us with the hope that he will be voted out of office on November 3. Having been left with a weak-minded solution to our catastrophic problem makes us complicit in the wasting of tens of thousands of innocent people before that date.

Several commentators and government officials, such as Speaker of the House Nancy Pelosi, have suggested, belatedly, that we turn to the provisions of that 25th Amendment I have written about a number of times in these newsletters and elsewhere. But they speak of such resort in connection with his recent contraction of the virus, whereas my references to that Amendment dealt with a preexisting mental aberration from which the president has suffered from his boyhood.* The question offers itself: Why have we delayed so long while people were dying every day in their thousands?

These so-called "debates" deserve some attention. If we persist in subjecting the public to these farcical performances, let them be conducted with some semblance of decorum and orderliness; as Webster would describe the presentation: "a regulated discussion…between two matched sides," rather than these tiresome, wrangling, interruptive sessions, to include the blatant lying with which these childish public displays have become common today. I have seen, heard, or read about these disorderly displays since their inception—those between the late JFK and his opponent, an unshaved criminal named Richard (Tricky Dick) Nixon, another blot on our presidential escutcheon. In the vice presidential "debate" on the 7th October, Mike Pence was clean-shaven, looked well, but perhaps owing to his innocent, almost honeyed behavior, if we couldn't say he drew flies, unquestionably he did draw a fly. And much in keeping with his entire lying performance, it did not fly but crawled around his head for the remainder of his act.

But there must be accountability, so I could suggest that prior to the debate and in public view (on TV) the opponents be sworn under oath, as are witnesses in all court proceedings, to tell the truth, and advised that if were caught lying they would be prosecuted for committing perjury, which would be made public, and suffer the penalty

---

* See Open Letter VII for an adequate explanation. *q.v.* Open Letters III, VIII, IX, X, XI, XIII, XVI and XVIII.

(three years prison in many states). Of course, they could find cover under the Fifth Amendment, which would be tantamount to an admission they otherwise would lie. Almost certainly if such strictures were placed on these so-called debates we would see an end to this laughable travesty altogether. Whatever happens, we'll never see or hear anything to compare with those Greek rhetoricians of the dim past or in modern history even those *comparatively decorous* engagements between Lincoln and Douglas.

Once more I think of Diogenes going through the streets of Athens looking for an honest man. A very old (but not ancient) Greek friend of mine and now a resident of the United States said this when I asked him what he thought of our president: "Honestly God! He is blastfamous!"

And so on to the man who would be king. Well, at least Kipling's character was honest enough to admit what he wanted. When Trump was medevacked to Walter Reed Medical Center a week or so ago, if I were disposed to condole with those Christian Evangelists who make up a substantial number of Trump's adherents I might remind them that, as William Cowper proclaimed, God moves in a mysterious way, his wonders to perform. When it was announced that the president was infected with the virus a week or so ago, the overly sentimental,* pro forma, and hypocritical pronouncements with which the news was accompanied, literally made me nauseous. Newscasters, commentators, and their guests wished the president well

---

* One of the "Bastard Muses" which, along with political correctness and the "I'm okay, you're okay" catch phrase, or byword, that also have come to plague us. See *A Sharp Seasoning of Truth, A Comprehensive Commentary in Pursuit of Genuine National Security,* 2019, by this author for a full explication.

and almost prayerfully hoped for his recovery. These were the same people who on CNN and other news outlets had been condemning him with every breath, unto claiming that he was a homicidal maniac who was directly responsible for hundreds of thousands of deaths. I call that a disgusting demonstration—inexplicable, indefensible, and hypocritical. Could this bizarre turnabout have been due to some latent, subliminal superstitious impulse, as in that old Latin tag, *de mortuis nihil nisi bonum* (of the dead [say] nothing but good), as a safeguard in the event of his succumbing to the virus for whose devastating consequences he himself was responsible? On my part, I prefer to hope (more honestly I'm pleased to say) that however long those steroids keep him standing, Donald Trump must pay his butcher's bill, perhaps hoist on his own petard.* If he isn't permanently disposed of by the virus or by losing the imminent election, we must invoke that 25th Amendment, somehow. Meanwhile, under his ambivalent mismanagement of aid to those who are pleading for it (Main, not Wall Street) millions of innocent (however misguided) citizens who thus far have managed to survive the deadly virus are jobless, homeless due to evictions for non-payment of rent or mortgages, and in some cases literally starving.†

---

* Centuries ago, when the besiegers of a castle, citadel, or other fortification needed ingress, their sappers or combat engineers, or whatever they were known as then, would be sent to emplace and detonate an explosive charge to breach a wall. The device they employed was called a *petard* (French for an expulsion of intestinal gas, viz. a fart), placed at the foot of a wall. If they didn't set the fuse properly they would be killed by their own device, bomb.

† Unimpeachable sources have revealed that *each day* in this country fourteen million children are not getting enough to eat.

And still this devil's disciple continues undeterred, reminding me once more of that shifty criminal in the old movie *Algiers*, who was compared to a clock that shows twelve, strikes two, when it is actually a quarter to four (I may not have the numbers right but I'm sure you get the point). Some fruits of his devilry on the domestic scene include the foiled plot to kidnap and perhaps kill the Governor of Michigan and the arrest of a dozen people involved in the plot who openly admitted that they were the forerunners of a rebellion; in foreign affairs, in addition to those crises I've already mentioned in a previous newsletter, Azerbaijan and Armenia now are at war (presently in a truce brokered by Russia). And with the able connivance of Trump's son-in-law Jared Kushner, relations between Israel and the Palestinians remain worse than ever. Not least of our foreign threats is ISIS, which Trump has claimed we have "eliminated 100 percent." ISIS is as alive and much of a threat *as it ever was*; *it merely* has reorganized into a horizontal, worldwide force.

One cardinal rule of expository writing is to produce paragraphs that are cohesive and comprehensive. In short, to focus upon and discuss adequately one facet of what subject the writer wants to explain or discuss. In this the twenty-sixth in this series of open letters I will ignore those rules. A paragraph in this piece may consist of merely a sentence, or it may be lengthy and larded with semicolons. The final product, using a term from the graphic arts, will be akin to a work of expressionism, a multifaceted collection of words, not images, of a large socio-political landscape, or perhaps a mosaic.

Our current situation has become so dire on both the public health and economic fronts that only a fool could think matters will improve eventually and that God will once again "shed His grace" on this "sweet land of liberty." But barring some sort of Divine Intervention we must find our own way out of the disastrous plight in which we find ourselves, much of it of our own making. We must separate ourselves from the fantasies our president would have us believe and cleave to the cold facts presented to us so insistently by medical science. But without authoritative leadership we will fail. At this point we can only rid ourselves of Trump and hope that former vice-president Biden will and can provide that leadership.

Two weeks from today, as I write this, the second and final presidential debate will be held. Unless the Debate Commission's technical staff can manage matters so that the moderator will be able to mute Trump's interruptions, harangues, and diatribes we will witness merely another of those verbal brawls we were subjected to in that first fiasco. But even if Trump's tiresome rambles could be controlled we shouldn't expect to see and hear anything like the Lincoln-Douglas debates or those well-regulated affairs at Oxford University, and this is to say nothing of those ancient Greek rhetoricians.

Having mentioned the Lincoln-Douglas debates brings to mind the matter of slavery, which comprised a major part of those Lincoln-Douglas encounters. In a brief digression from current political matters, let me offer this for your consideration. For many years after the Civil War many Americans, mainly Southerners, would have it that the war was precipitated by a disagreement over states' rights. Others, in great part Northerners, held that the war was fought over the narrower more moral question of slavery *per se* (and since the civil rights movement, the latter cause has been accepted as the overriding one). If you reflect upon what I've written about the Americans' obsession with wealth—our almost reverential worship of the Great God Mammon—I think you may see my position. I think the origins of the Civil War are not to be found in any question of the states' rights nor entirely in the moral aspects of the long-standing practice of slavery. Rather, they are to be found mainly in the cold, practical province of economics, more specifically, profits.

Those plantation owners in the South were enjoying their heyday. Cotton was King, and they had established large markets not only in the northern United States but in Europe, mainly in England and France. Here at home those textile mills and dry goods manufacturers in the North especially provided a lucrative and conveniently accessible outlet for those cotton bales. Slavery provided greater profits all around: low-cost production on those plantations (no wages and minimal subsistence for the slaves) and thus lower prices for those consumers at home and abroad. So much for what I hope was a profitable (in both senses) digression.

But back to the perils of our current dismal affairs. Our only hope for the near future lies in Biden's replacement of President Trump, and let us hope that the coming election proves to be a relatively straightforward process, uncomplicated and unchallenged by one or more of Trump's "Heads I win, tails you lose" scurvy ploys. Trump, who with his last-minute, almost frantic and ill-considered rallies and with his threats of refusing to accept defeat in the coming election, should by now be a laughing stock. All that prevents right-thinking people from seeing him as such is the almost mystifying allegiance paid him by those millions of hard core supporters who stubbornly refuse to see him as the dangerous lunatic he in fact is. Those crowds of diehard Trump supporters at these latter-day, desperate rallies, in their almost trancelike disregard of all the sound medical advice about trying to mitigate the spread of the virus seem almost hypnotized in their unquestioning belief in whatever Trump propounds, however blatantly untrue and outrageous. Like so many lambs going docily to the slaughter, their unshakable faith in this egomaniac is almost beyond belief. In their fanaticism I'm reminded of what Clarence Darrow faced when confronted during that "monkey trial" in Tennessee in 1925 with William Jennings Bryan and his fervid followers, who were convinced that the earth was only six thousand years old.*

Putting all that side, if Biden becomes president we should not expect a swift or even lasting relief from all our problems. Does Biden have the ability to deal with the incredibly difficult problems with which we are faced, both domestically and abroad, that are the result of Trump's ineptitude in general and not least in his mishandling the great pandemic we have been and will continue to endure for an inestimable period of time? Will he have the stamina and longevity necessary to see the task through? Will his advisers be well-intended people of integrity who will be dedicated to the public's best interests rather than to those lobbyists on "K" Street and those financiers on Wall Street? Then there is the longer view of our future. I find it difficult if not impossible to believe that even if we are fortunate enough to weather this great storm, rid ourselves of the pox and restabilize our economic and financial affairs, that no matter how noble Biden's intentions or even those of his successors, Capitalism, that symbiotic interrelationship, that sinister triumvirate—governmental-business; business news media; and government-news media—will not reassert itself. Of one thing I am pleased, however small the consolation, and it is that after almost three years of campaigning, the election is only a couple of weeks away. The TV industry has pocketed billions of dollars in campaign spending,

---

* Somewhat less than the four billion years that scientists have proven and the rest of the world is convinced of.

mainly financed by the big corporations who will collect if their candidate wins and takes office (revisit the Great God Mammon and the "triumvirate," above). Three years, while in all other countries campaigns last a matter of weeks.

In an earlier letter I suggested that some Americans might have had enough of all this ineptitude and uncertainty and yes, even fear, and so might decide to emigrate to another country. Now I could propose as an alternative on a much grander scale, that accepting as a consensus we were all wrong about the revolution and trying to establish a democratic form of governance, and as an alternative to "fleeing the scene" of this frightful pandemic, that we should consider asking the Brits (despite their diminished stature on the world's stage) if they would consider reinstating us, so to speak, in some capacity, as part of the royal realm, perhaps much as was the status of India under the Raj prior to 1947.

I f only, just for a moment and simultaneously, all the world's leaders realized just what we are doing to this planet and what the inevitable result. Of course such a collective epiphany is a fantasy; unless by some Divine intervention that should happen. I'm talking about climate change, specifically global warming, with its inexorable and grim consequences. If I weren't one of the laziest people who ever stood up in shoeleather I would verify that I've said this in an earlier letter, but as I know I have said that some things are worth repeating, I'll say it here. If in verifying the result in the 2000 presidential election the Supreme Court hadn't decided in favor of "Mission Accomplished" Bush, the inevitable result of climate change might have been forestalled to some extent. If Al Gore had been elected president and been voted in for a second term we would be at least eight years ahead of where we are now. Mother Nature is implacable and relentless and we've done nothing significant to avoid the inevitable: Life as we know it will no longer exist on this planet. Serious action now, on a global scale would come too late to avert the coming catastrophe. As only one indication of what is happening, we already have experienced 25 hurricanes (mid-October 2020) along the Gulf Coast. The record breaking fires in the West speak for themselves, while cities and towns along the East Coast are being inundated. Miami beach is already at sea level and Miami itself soon will have water running in its streets. In the foreseeable future "moving with glacial speed" (as in Congress conducting the peoples' affairs) will become a dead metaphor since they (glaciers, not Congressmen, unfortunately) are fast disappearing. An ice field the size of Rhode Island has already broken away from the Antarctic icepack. Although I have seen authoritative reports based on sound science describing what we can expect (those of us who survive the pandemic) in the not too distant and dismal future, I won't share it with you here. Those of you who read probably can get the essence of it online with your "magic phones."

President Trump is a prime example of the "leaders" I spoke of. In his callous and aberrant dismissal of the global death-trap we are facing he can be said to be the patron saint of this mind set. The fact that the majority of world leaders are elderly makes the forlorn hope that I fantasized about at the beginning of this newsletter even more unlikely. Why should these people care what happens twenty years from now? Trump is seventy-four years old. Added to that fact his total lack of empathy and his unpredictability make any hope profitless. Compared to this man a loose cannon (a runaway muzzle loader on the deck of a pitching, rolling, and yawing sailing ship of yore) looks like a well-secured piece of orderly ordnance. And should anything happen to this paragon of virtue to prevent him from carrying on as president, that rubber stamp of a Vice President would be no improvement. Mike Pence is the epitome of what once was said about all vice presidents: You could take him out and bury him in the Rose Garden and no one would miss him for six months.

Losing Ruth Bader Ginsberg from the Supreme Court will have serious and long lasting consequences. The timing of her death was a classic example of the devil's own work, he who himself seems to be operating, however clandestinely, within the precincts of the White House. Despite the lying pronouncements made by Lindsay Graham during the Obama administration about not holding any hearings on Supreme Court appointments during a presidential election year Graham now is doing his level best as Chairman of the Senate Judiciary Committee to do what he once swore never to do. Now, with the urging of Trump and Senate Majority Leader McConnell, Graham is setting a new record in seeing through the Senate's approval of Trump nominee Amy Coney Barrett. The Committee will approve her (while the Democrats will boycott the hearing). The full Senate will approve her on the 26th October, and she should be seated on the Court the next day. Unless Biden becomes the next President, the Democrats win a majority in the Senate and maintain their majority in the House, and this results in legislation to increase the number of justices, the Court will be in the hands of the far right conservatives, with a vindictive and gleeful Trump dancing in the wings even if he loses the presidency. If he wins another term the Court will just move more quickly to vote favorably for the decisions he and his cohorts have been lusting for. Whatever happens we won't enjoy one of the best qualities of our democracy that goes back to the founding fathers of this country, and that is the peaceful transfer of power.

With control in the hands of the Trumped up assemblage of adjudicators Alito, Gorsuch, Kavanaugh, Rubber Stamp Thomas and now Barrett in the majority, unless Chief Justice Roberts sides with them, the liberal Briers, Sottomayor, and Kagan will lose every case brought before the Court, and Trump will still be dictating to the Court as a lame duck president. What cases? The Affordable Care Act, which is scheduled to come before the Court on 10th November; Roe v. Wade; DACA and immigration-citizenship in general; gun control; voters' rights; unjust law enforcement cases; and this is to say nothing about cases that may be brought before the Court springing from Trump's calamitous handling of the pandemic, foreign affairs, and relations. So whatever the outcome of the election we won't be out of the woods until next year, if ever we are.

Trump's personal relation with Putin and the Russians is unclear. We know that he was negotiating with someone or some entity in Moscow about building a "Trump Tower" (possibly a hotel) but that seems insufficient to explain the deference he has shown to Putin and the Russians generally. Could there be any justification for that seemingly outrageous claim made by former British MI6 agent Christopher Steele to Julian Assange of WikiLeaks? According to Steele a videotape exists, of which the Russians have a copy, showing Trump, while in the Company of two Putin provided prostitutes, watching as they urinated on one another while cavorting on the bed former President Obama and his wife slept in while on a visit to Moscow in 2013. Ah well, as the old saying goes, however smooth and fair the skin, stench and corruption lie within, and I include my apologies to those of you whose skin is of a color other than "fair."

The only way for evil to triumph is for Good Men to do Nothing. Seemingly our last hope of ridding ourselves of that plague spot on the pages of our nation's history is Edmund Burke's reflection. Let us pray that there are enough good men, and women, to vote Trump out of office.

October 31, 2020

Is our situation hopeless? I won't vouch for our chances of surviving the onslaught of climate change and its frightful implications,[*] but barring that horror perhaps there is some hope. One thing is certain: we should not spend what time we may have left wallowing in fear. Though they are extremely rare, "miracles" are known to have occurred. So let's light up one or two of the dark corners and a few other dim areas of that large canvas I have been revealing to you.

The presidential election that will take place a few days from now is fraught with uncertainties and potential conflict. To express merely one possibility, one can hope that our *Führer* (Trump) doesn't send his "Brown Shirts"[†] to the polling stations to bully and intimidate any Biden voters they may be able to identify.

In the imminent election, however much it may be pervaded by Trump's scurvy tricks, the Jewish Americans will be faced with an additional dilemma to the one all

---

[*] Too late we must face the reality that Mother Nature is a tangible force and not just something we can manipulate to satisfy our own selfish desires.
[†] Hitler's organization of thugs used before and after he became Chancellor of Germany in 1933 to suppress his opponents.

Americans must contend with (controlling the pandemic-reopening the economy), and if you'll permit me to coin a phrase, I call it Trump versus Trump. On average, Jews are some of the most intelligent people on earth (they invented the modern system of banking six hundred years ago), and the great majority of them are right-minded people, except for a significant number who are conflicted and ambivalent between loyalty to their adoptive home, the United States, and the State of Israel; perhaps more precisely the *idea* of the existence of an Israel, after two thousand years of persecution throughout their history and throughout the world. Whatever that case, there remains the fact that though Jews comprise less than three percent of the total population of the U.S., their influence in elections is disproportionately significant, especially under the Electoral College system of tabulating votes.

Jewish Americans tend to be concentrated in certain areas, not least in the densely populated areas in a handful of states; California, New York, Illinois, and Florida, where their influence can be decisive. And they vote, which is not the least important consideration here. When Israel declared herself a sovereign state on 15 May 1948 and hastened to get official U.S. approval of her declaration, Harry Truman, who had no especial love for Jews in general, was reminded by an old co-worker in that haberdashery in Kansas that he consider very seriously the fact that a presidential election would take place in six months. Truman picked up his phone and gave his approval and blessing then and there to the newly established "sovereign" state.

The vast majority of Jews in this country hold views that are either antithetical or indifferent to those of

Trump's hard core followers, whom he has frightened sufficiently to see him, despite his outrageous behaviors, their only hope of protection from their worst fears: Black crime in general and now specifically in the white suburbs; a collective consensus condemning the ideology of white supremacy; overwhelming immigration; Jews in general ("they are running the country"); gun control; abortion rights; and all liberals. There must be others, but I'm sure you get the idea.

Now Trump, who though cunning probably has an IQ that matches his age, under the tutelage of his scheming son-in-law Jared Kushner, an ardent political Zionist, and others who share the same political views, has demonstrated a support for Israel unequalled by any of his predecessors—moving the U.S. Embassy from Tel Aviv to Jerusalem is only one example. So where is this dilemma I spoke of? That should have made itself apparent by now. The Jews in this country know Trump for what he is, and for what he is doing to this country, not least the economy, as do any clear-thinking, sensible people. Biden, if he's said anything about U.S.-Israel relations, has said very little. But even if he doesn't commit himself before the election, I think the great majority of U.S. Jews will vote for him, and hoping that if he doesn't exhibit unequivocal support for the Israelis, he will treat the relationship no worse nor better than it was during the Obama-Biden administration. Jews may not be sure about Biden, but they enjoy the benefits this country still has to offer them, their names are not excluded from the COVID-19 casualty lists, and they're fully aware that it's time to empty the trash at the White House. Reflect upon how many Jewish-American medical and other scientific experts as well as other lay sociopolitical commentators have appeared on the TV news outlets, all of whom have condemned Trump and his staff for the insane mishandling of the pandemic from its very beginning.

So Trump and his gang of miscreants go on, virtually ignoring the body count due to this overwhelming scourge. We have heard that power corrupts; I'm beginning to believe that it also can cause a kind of lunacy. Vice President Pence has the additional Constitutional duty of serving as the President of the Senate. He now has announced that if (when) Amy Coney Barrett comes before the entire Senate for approval to serve as a Supreme Court Justice he will seat himself as Senate President. The full Senate hearing should occur during one of the few days remaining before the election. Meanwhile, at least five of the Vice President's personal staff have tested positive for the virus. Despite this, Pence insists on attending and presiding over the hearing rather than quarantining himself, as medical protocol would require him to do. If Pence, who like his leader seldom wears a mask or practices social distancing, somehow introduces the pox to other members of the Senate let us hope that those infected will be Republicans.

I have said little about the importance of the Senate and its power among the three branches of government. Even if Biden were to replace Trump he would to an important degree be impeded in his stated intentions of bringing the nation together as the true union it should be, without the bitter partisan divisions we have seen increasingly, especially under the current administration. Leader Mitch McConnell and his adherents in the senior chamber of Congress have battened on Trump's contempt for the democratic liberals. If those Democrats retake control of the Senate, it will make Biden's path much easier. Therefore voters should not neglect the bottom part of their ballots, where a number of Republican Senators are seeking reelection.

The ship of state, after a long voyage fraught with storms and other perils, having clawed its way off a lea shore ridden with reefs and shoals, and more or less intact, has arrived at a relatively safe port of call. Yes, I'm speaking of the results of the recent presidential election and my amazement that now, after what President Trump has put this country and its inhabitants through during the past four years, he and his supporters and enablers in both Congress and in the general populace are being permitted to question, *legally,* its outcome. Biden received 306 electoral college votes while Trump acquired only 232 of the 270 needed to win reelection. And Biden set a new all-time record of more than 78 million popular votes beating Trump's by five and one half million. As important is the fact that Biden turned Arizona and Georgia "blue," both of which have been Republican strongholds (red states) for decades. Moreover, Biden's Democrats are counting on the possibility, bordering more on probability each day, that the Democrat candidates in the latter state will be victorious in winning the run-off election to be held on December 5th, thus giving them a majority in the Senate and leaving Trump's cat's paw Majority Leader Mitch McConnell "beached," along with a number of Trump's other loudmouthed Senate lackeys. One can only hope that those candidates in that Georgia run-off win, and that the Democrats in the House retain their majority (and for the edification of those of you who may be wondering, I'm neither a Democrat nor a Republican, both of whom, even in the best of times, are held in thrall by the big money interests in this country). All this bitter infighting and unavailing partisanship during a time when the corona virus not merely is spreading exponentially but astronomically, killing innocent citizens and those who would wish to be citizens alike in their hundreds of thousands.

In 2016 Trump boasted that he could murder some one with impunity on Park Avenue. Today he could make the same pronouncement about the quarter of a million people for whose death he bears responsibility during the last ten months. But Trump and his seventy million adherents, who like limpets or barnacles cling to the hull of that ship of state, continue to insist on their baseless claims of fraudulent practices while virtually ignoring what is probably the greatest threat this nation has faced since it won its independence.

If it weren't for that archaic and benighted electoral college system (established 220 years ago by the Constitution), our history books would have to be revised as to the names of our presidents. The outcomes of a number of presidential elections would be reversed, especially in our recent history. And who can say that the reversing of these "split decisions" would not have been to our benefit? To cite just a few examples: If Wilkie* had beaten Roosevelt in 1940 would we

---

* I recall an FDR campaign button of that era that read: A horse's tail is long and silky; lift it up and you'll see Wilkie.

have declared war on Germany at Churchill's urging while reeling from Japan's attack on Pearl Harbor? Would we have attacked Iraq in 2003, spurred on by Bush's muddleheaded and specious claims of *casus belli*? With Gore at the helm we would be eight years ahead of where we now find ourselves in staving off the overwhelming spectre of global warming;* and finally, although Hillary Clinton may not have been the answer to our domestic problems (Wall Street, inequitable distribution of wealth) she learned something about foreign affairs as Secretary of State and in the White House when her libidinous husband was president. In any case, she won the popular vote†, but thanks to that infernal electoral college her opponent won the election, and the rest of us have lost pretty much everything that's worth having in this once beautiful country of ours; except perhaps for hope, and even that is beginning to wear a little thin. The incumbent Charlatan has spoken for himself.

As I've said elsewhere, we are long overdue for the holding of a Constitutional convention. Aside from this matter of that sadly outdated electoral college there are

---

* Truly, an extinction event; not moving as quickly as being struck by a large meteor, asteroid or a comet, but an extinction event nonetheless.

† *Vox populi, vox Dei* (the voice of the people is the voice of God). Act II of the Constitution provides that electors should equal the total number of Congressional representatives from a state, i.e., its two Senators and the number of Representatives to Congress. So if the populace of a "red" or "blue" state declare for their party's candidate, all that state's electoral votes go to that candidate and the popular vote becomes meaningless. This is akin, in an obverse way perhaps, to the apportionment of Senators. Since the time of the thirteen colonies certain states have grown apace while others are sparsely populated. Montana's population of less than a million is sparse compared to California's forty million, but each sends two Senators to Washington, with equal voting power.

other changes that cry out to be made; not least is that Second Amendment to the Bill of Rights which through its scandalous and willful misinterpretation by all three branches of our government has been responsible for the needless deaths and injuries to innocent people, not least our children, in the tens of thousands annually. The Constitutional "originalists" such as the late Antonin Scalia, who mentored the latest appointee to the Supreme Court, Amy Coney Barret, herself a rigid advocate of the letter of the law, *as written*, of that (to them) sacred document, should be placed in a time machine, were one available, and sent back to the year 1798.* Biden can only hope that our judicial branch has the integrity and the spirit to decide for the public good.

As a short "sidebar" to all this, should the recount President Trump has demanded in Arizona verify Joe Biden as the winner there, we might say that the dead hand of the late Senator John McCain reached in, seeking justice for himself and for his fellow guests at the "Hanoi Hilton." In the meantime Russia continues to amplify Trump's specious charges of election fraud while Iran and Israel wonder what the Biden administration will bring.†

In speaking of revising the Constitution, I could have added that this interregnum between Biden's clear victory and his inauguration on January 20th 2021 is inordinately long. Trump himself is proving that even as a "lame duck" he can do considerable harm. Instead of mending the corrosive division between the two political sides he is

---

* Man's laws do not enjoy the immutability of Holy Writ; they were written by man, for man.

† While the rest of the world expresses clear relief.

strengthening and prolonging it. A willing, cooperative, and peaceful transfer of power, with both sides honestly intent on the welfare of the country as a whole instead battling bitterly for political preeminence is not to be hoped for as it has in executive transmissions in the past, and the nation's security at home as well as that abroad may well suffer for it. As only one grim example are those top secret contingency plans I once was privileged to work with*. Another is vital information about the pandemic, which is a more immediate threat. Trump's diehards, at his direction undoubtedly, refuse to share with Biden's transition team, especially during this devastating pandemic, and this could seal the fate of the United States as the leader of the free world. Instead of the prescribed ten weeks (on average) that presumes a tranquil and productive transfer of power with the benefits of continued security (assuming we are and have been enjoying such a state, particularly after the outrages the Trump administration has visited upon us during the last four years) the transition should be accomplished in a couple of weeks. Of course in that exalted period when we had achieved our independence, the founders could not even conceive that anyone such as a Donald Trump could possibly have been voted into our highest office. As Marc Antony said over Caesar's body, "The good men do dies with them; the evil that men do lives after them." Typical of Trump's foul depredations is his enjoining his staff (what's left of them) to devise a way in which he could *pardon himself* in the event of his being indicted and convicted of some high crime or misdemeanor

---

* The least Trump could do would be to give Biden, whose security clearance must still be valid, the nuclear activation codes.

after leaving office and becoming a private citizen again. Meanwhile, knowing that most Democrats don't like to engage in violence, except to watch it on TV, millions of Trump supporters can be heard loading and cocking their weapons. Trump refuses to concede to Biden's victory, and those millions of his adherents who have settled in his cat's cradle of deceit with benign acceptance are beginning to stir. Protests on his behalf have already begun in the nation's capital and probably will spread to other cities. Still, there is a glimmer of hope that a significant number of Republican Senators will break with him and even threaten to vote with Democrat members of Congress if he continues to deny the reality of his failing to achieve a second term.

Not so much of a novel perhaps but a good short story which contains all the elements that raise some of those tales above others of their kind could be plotted and presented about the current political situation on a personal level. Suppose one of Trump's staunchest supporters, one who remains close to him not merely in his insane actions and pronouncements, but in close physical proximity, as would a bodyguard, realizes that his idol's feet were merely made of clay; that his assertions and promises were totally insincere, mere lies for his own benefit and only intended to keep him in power. Imagine further that this same almost fanatically loyal supporter's entire family—wife, children, his own parents—all died that lonely death insisted upon by the virus they all contracted after their attendance at one of those celebrated Trump political rallies. See finally how in a fit of betrayed rage this once beguiled, trusted, and dedicated retainer assassinates his false Caesar in public view....

There's the Treatment; you can write the story if you would wish to.

But such poetic justice that one may wish for seldom happens, so I'll give you this bit of realism. Recently President elect Biden was quoted as saying, and I paraphrase, If we delay in taking some action in this pandemic (while Trump refuses to concede his loss in the election and won't permit the transition teams to meet) more people *may* die…. The italics are mine and the word should be *will*. With two months until the inauguration, at the present rate of one thousand per day, at least 60,000 *will* die. As long as Trump retains the title of President and keeps his supporters in thrall, not least those pusillanimous Republicans in the Senate, the killing of these innocent people will continue. However indirectly, Trump has been and will continue to be guilty of homicide *en masse*. We waited and vacillated until the election, hoping we could rid ourselves of this excrescence by that process. We failed. Now the new vaccines have taken center stage, and Trump will take full credit for this. But there remains the fact that before they become available and are distributed, two or three hundred thousand more people may have died.

Add to this that Trump still is the Commander-in-Chief of all U.S. armed forces. As such, along with the withdrawal from Iraq and Afghanistan, he has now threatened to order a strike against one of Iran's nuclear development sites. With Iran's arch enemy Israel and her arsenal of nuclear weapons in the Negev Desert, such a strike as proposed by Trump could, to use a pungent metaphor by the late Edward Said, be the spark that lights the fuse of a third world war. How much harm can one man do? Do we have another nascent

Napoleon or a Hitler to deal with? Are we to continue to permit him to wreak havoc and devastation from an office at 1600 Pennsylvania Avenue? Although Donald may be a lame duck, he's anything but a harmless one.

Meanwhile, this *danse macabre* goes on, seemingly without end. A most troubling thought I have about our near future, as is that about global warming in the not too distant future, is the portentous fact that seventy-one million Americans voted for Trump in the recent election. The majority of these voting adults comprise almost one fifth of our adult population and have proven to be unshakeable in their fealty and outspoken support of their demagogue in the White House. To cite a crude analogy, one thinks of those abolitionists pitted against the Solid South in the mid-nineteenth century. Yes, as unimaginable as it may seem we might be on the verge of not a fully fledged civil war (the "Trumpeters," spread out across the nation and lacking organizational cohesiveness couldn't rise to that level of belligerence), a "patchwork" rebellion. If such were to come to pass this might be a good time to begin restricting the sale of small arms ammunition. We couldn't do anything about the more than 300 million weapons in civilian hands out there, to say nothing about those in the thousands of national guard and army reserve armories throughout the fifty states.

There will be those of you who may feel that I have cast a pall of darkness and hopelessness over our citizens and even humankind generally. You would be quite justified in doing so. We as a nation are proving, as did the ancient Greeks, that *true* democracy is extremely difficult to achieve; there are those political scientists who are convinced that it is impossible. So let's say that democracy as it exists today is but a poor best among governmental forms that have been tried and failed. Communism, as Karl Marx envisioned it, really was a wonderful idea, in theory. So was fascism if it had been enlightened dictatorship. But those who implemented those governmental forms failed to consider the fatal and inevitable flaw in such systems— the human factor, the human frailty of vulnerability and susceptibility to those seven deadly sins I spoke of earlier in this work. Somewhat ironically, in view of what the Nazis put Europe through, this German maxim is apt: *Aus so krummen Holz, als woraus der Mensch gemacht ist kann nichts ganz Gerades gezimmert worden.* Out of the crooked timber of humanity no straight thing can ever be made, or to put it more simply, you can't make a good pot out of poor clay. And this applies to the character and integrity of both groups: the governors and the governed. On the side of the former there too often is the lust for power, perhaps wealth, or the pursuit of a personal agenda, or perhaps all of these. On that of the latter are indifference, apathy, lethargy, selfishness, indolence, and not least, ignorance. Winston Churchill once said words to this effect: "Democracy is a bad choice of government, but it's the best we have."

One of democracy's perils as we practice it is our own persistence in selecting some of the worst examples of popular representation possible. Former President Trump, and to a slightly lesser extent, Senate Minority Leader Mitch McConnell and House Minority Leader Kevin McCarthy are just three with which you will be familiar; as to the dozens of others now in the Congress, I never expected to see such self-seeking cowards. It is not enough to tell the public (if that public is even paying attention), repeatedly and futilely, that Trump was the causative element in the runaway scourge of a pandemic that has killed more than 600,000 Americans thus far and who now has become the main cause of the destructive divisiveness among our people to a point where he makes Huey Long seem like a lonely voice crying in the wilderness. How long will it take to rid ourselves of him? Perhaps never, if the shadow of his demagoguery still looms over those 75,000,000 people who voted for him in the last presidential election and their progeny after he is gone, somehow. We may have to cope with the damage he has done and will continue to do to our already flawed and inequitable state of capitalistic democracy—winner take all, disappearance of a true middle class, actual poverty in a significant portion of our populace. Can we, through a combined effort of intellect, will, and perseverance find a way to control ourselves individually and collectively so as to achieve a state of self-imposed stability, security, and serenity in our social pursuits? Can we do this while at the same time those millions of unseeing Trump acolytes seem to be on the verge of constituting a third party of fanatical zealots? To say that America's form of democracy, touted for the world to see and hear, and that its Constitution is the oldest and most durable in history, has become laughable is not too strong a statement. Our Constitution is flawed and obsolescent, and I will speak more of this in due course. Meanwhile the waves of adversity are breaking farther and farther upon the shore and eroding the earth this country was founded upon beneath our very feet, and we seem to have no means to halt this inexorable destruction.

In a recent interview with Barack Obama, CNN's Anderson Cooper asked: "Do you think we're teetering on the brink of crisis?" Good Lord! Does he not see that we're *in* crisis now, and have been since the last Presidential election? In fact, we now are faced with numerous *crises* which overlap each other. What we *are* teetering on is the brink of collapse. So if we're overdue for a drastic change, what kind of governance would suit our needs? News outlets give us repetitiously the journalistic who, what, when, where, how, etc., but seldom *the true why of the matter* and, as important, that other *what (to do)*. As Lenin wrote in his little book, *What is to be Done?* over a hundred years ago, we must ask ourselves what is to be done about the crises we face today.

But before we try to answer that question let's look at some of the cardinal crises in the paradigm. If we are honest and unsparing in our criticism, we will see why our system of capitalist democracy now is in total disarray. It is failing because the means to make it reasonably successful that should be inherent in the system itself are lacking. In short, our system of governance has become its own worst enemy.

The COVID-19 pandemic provides a classic example of this, with its conflict between states' rights and Federal (national) necessity. Aside from Trump's blundering, self-seeking bravado was the lack of control and stringent mandates needed, and which the Executive Branch of our central government failed to provide. In a word, what was needed was strength from above—mandates, *orders*, with suitable penalties for non-compliance. With such central control quite probably hundreds of thousands of lives could have been spared. While the White House dithered and Trump insouciantly lied about the true seriousness of the virus, the states, desperate for the medical supplies, personnel, and facilities to control the outbreak (there were no adequate stockpiles at the state or federal level) entered into a bidding war with one another with supplies going to the highest bidder (and the stock market continued to rise, while the corpses continued to fill the reefer trailers in hospital parking lots because the morgues were full). The pandemic hasn't ended, and the "D" type virus, which already comprises sixty percent of the cases reported and is sixty percent more communicable than the type "A" we originally had to contend with, is rising steadily. Still, though the vaccines currently in use have proven to be effective against this latest variable, there are millions of people who for a variety of reasons haven't and probably won't get vaccinated. To date, less than fifty percent of those who are eligible to be vaccinated are completely vaccinated. We now have five "hot spot" clusters mainly in the southern U.S. The longer that "D" virus can spread, the more likely a new variant will develop and we will be back where we started in defeating COVID-19. On Wall Street, stocks have already begun to tumble as concerns over the Delta variant rise. In June 2021, 100 percent of deaths reported in Maryland were attributed to the new virus. Meanwhile epidemiologists are predicting yet another surge of the disease in late summer and early fall of 2021, (back to school time) which by that time almost undoubtedly will be dominated by that highly contagious "D" variety or perhaps worse, its successor of the current scourge. Despite all this, unvaccinated people increasingly are attending crowded public events, or flying or driving all over the country, or sailing around aimlessly on those huge cruise ships, and so on. Once again politics has drawn a shroud over our very destiny.

By invoking a war powers act—we've heard enough times that we're fighting a war against however unseen an enemy and with more than 600,000 already dead, could this horror not be described as an invasion by a deadly enemy?—much of the incompetence, indecision, and unnecessary expense (think of the Office of Price Administration and price-fixing in World War II) could have been avoided. And instead of suggesting, cajoling, and even bribing citizens to get vaccinated—beer and wine given free in New Jersey, million-dollar lotteries in Ohio, Leidos, a vaccine producer, is offering a year's pay to employees who get vaccinated(!), joints for jabs (marijuana cigarettes) somewhere else, all as inducements to get vaccinated; and another reason why other nations see us as a laughing stock. A war powers act, if a war powers act seems inappropriate to some of you, try an emergency powers act, or a pandemic act, whatever you think is most appropriate-would authorize the federal government to make mandatory certain actions, with adequate penalties for failure to do so. Propagandists know too well that an attitudinal change is useless unless it leads to a behavioral change. The War Powers Act invoked during World War II directed, in part, to "raise, organize, equip, and *command* the necessary public forces, and *to apply such regulations affecting personal liberty* and the national economy as the exigencies may require." The italics are mine. So in this emergency, people could also be required to carry a valid shot record affirming their having been vaccinated. Whatever else we may do we must *enforce* a vaccination requirement.

The term "gun control" has become a meaningless misnomer. There is no gun control, nor will there be unless some drastic legal action is taken. Realizing that the solution to the infamous shootings that now have become bewildering in their frequency, could never be found by some way of getting the guns out of the hands of their civilian owners. Some other means must be attempted. There now are more firearms out there than people. By outright confiscation or by offering rewards for their voluntary relinquishment[*] would be virtually impossible. The solution could lay in rendering the weapons harmless. As a camera without film can produce no photos, so a gun without ammunition is useless, unless it is an obsolete military service rifle to which a bayonet can be fixed. But there would be little or no problem with that either since those who are doing the shooting are mainly

---

[*] As in our drive westward to achieve our "Manifest Destiny," Native Americans were told, "turn in your guns, your Government will take care of you." Then they "took care of them."

craven cowards who would want to avoid any close combat[*]. Restriction of certain types of ammunition (along with heavy penalties for non-compliance) could be accomplished with the stroke of a pen under a war powers act, even if it meant nationalization of the arms and ammunition companies who have been making fortunes out of the peculiar obsession with guns in this country, which the rest of the world views with astonishment and not a little repugnance.

Although I have had no close acquaintance with the later generation of small arms since I left the army years ago, some things change relatively slowly and experts are everywhere who could provide the technical information needed for the implementation of such a mandate. One thing hasn't changed in decades: the Colt Armalite AR-15 is still a favorite with civilian shooters. Upon acceptance in the army inventory, this weapon became the M16 service rifle (actually it's more of a carbine), and though inferior to Russia's AK47, still is a very lethal weapon. And I know it uses 5.56mm or .223 caliber ammunition. As for hand guns, including those which can accommodate large quantities of rounds in their magazines, 9mm pistol ammunition is almost universal; revolvers are not as popular as those semiautomatic pistols or the machine pistols, which can be converted to fully automatic by the removal of a little item called a sear, since (at least in this country) they can hold only five or six rounds of ammunition.

To achieve success with such a true gun control program, planning must be made for its implementation and not least

---

[*] See Terence Stamp in the rôle of British Sergeant Troy performing the sabre drill in the film adaptation of Thomas Hardy's *Far From the Madding Crowd*.

for its execution. A lesser but still important benefit, like the creation of the TSA (Transportation Safety Administration) in response to the 9/11 attack, is that of opening a significant number of new jobs. Of course provisions would have to be made for supplying adequate ammunition to the police and our armed forces. Meanwhile, rather than hearing about the root cause of the problem—guns and the lack of their control, we hear about motives and investigations, while flags are half-staffed, eulogies are given about the victims, hearts, minds, and prayers go out to the victim's families, and so on. But words aren't enough, any more than the balloons, the flowers at the scene, or the vigil candles lit after dark. No more are counselors made available to the mourners of the dead. All of this becomes meaningless in the face of the true cause of all this avoidable slaughter. And with Trump's misguided minions milling about threateningly, unless we're very careful we could be facing another civil war. Much as a lack of compromise may lead to war between nations, so it can between states and the central government on the domestic scene, and such unyielding partisanship as we now are experiencing may well produce another civil war. And many of those millions of firearms I spoke of unfortunately are in the hands of those millions of diehard Trump followers. And if I'm right, we would be wise to ensure (quietly and without any publicity) the loyalty to the central government of the states' militias, especially those states with Republican governors, and of course our own national armed forces, then pray that they are on the side of the angels; the alternative doesn't bear thinking about.[*]

---

[*] Here you may put me down as an alarmist, but through my long life I have found it useful, even crucial, to be careful about certain matters.

The opiate (now opioid) problem has reached and passed the crisis stage. I can offer no solution to this problem because it is such a personal and individual one. I can only suggest that there will be no solution until Americans begin to take what life has to offer them without their inclinations toward self-pity and their striving for happiness where there is none to be found. Without that, the problem will remain and will even worsen. Anti-depression pills now are the third biggest seller among licit drugs in this country.

With a population comprising less than five percent that of the world, we consume sixty-five percent of the illicit drugs that are sold. But however much most politicians place the cause of this other epidemic on the dealers who have found the United States to be the most lucrative market in the world, drug traffic will continue, based simply on that old economic principle of supply and demand.

Racism is still with us and in these Trumpian times may be stronger than ever. However, due to the efforts of the progressive Democrats (political correctness) "the great amalgamation" will remain a forlorn hope and will continue to do so until either intermarriage, or more likely, miscegenation of some kind over a period of time causes every human to look similar, at least as to skin color. This process, *sui generis*, will take time. Sooner than later, perhaps in a hundred years, our skin color, all of us, will be of a rich *caffé au lait* shade. We're already hearing phrases such as "The Browning of America," and the title of W. Kamau Bell's TV documentary, *The United Shades of America*. Later there may even evolve a similarity in physiognomy and other physical characteristics—no longer will the millennia-old accepted occidental standards of beauty, especially those of women, be based upon refined noses, silken hair, often blond, lips sensuous but not overly generous, high cheek bones, slender shapely legs, and so on. I'm no anthropologist, so I wouldn't even hazard a guess as to how long that additional change would take—a thousand years, ten thousand? But until such a change should occur, assuming it would occur at all, racism simply will have to be accepted as an ineradicable societal fact, however inequitable. Of course, all this is assuming that there is any living thing on this planet by that time due to climate change. And we must endure the virtually predictable result that our own forefathers visited upon us for self-seeking reasons of wealth and status in their "classless" new world. I suppose I must include myself despite the fact that though my forefathers may have been guilty of other sins, they couldn't be found guilty of this one. And racial prejudice went beyond this without going into the horrors perpetrated against the Native Americans, and those Chinese Exclusion Acts of the 1920s. Then more subtly perhaps, at least generally, was the prejudice against the southern Europeans, Slavs, Jews, anyone who wasn't a WASP (White Anglo-Saxon Protestant). Even the Irish were included, those who came in their thousands when their potato crop failed in the mid-nineteenth century; then in the late nineteenth century and continuing into the twentieth when hordes of down-trodden, indigent emigrants from all over Europe, not least the Jews who were escaping the pogroms in Russia and Poland. I have already gone into the matter of those wretched Mexicans and other central Americans on our southern border.

Yes, racism still exists, but in less open, less "honest" forms. You won't see patrons in movie houses enjoying Al

Jolson or Fred Astair or even Shirley Temple in blackface, or laughing at the antics of Stepin Fetchit and Butterfly McQueen, or listening to "Amos and Andy" (both actors were white men) on the radio in the evening. You won't hear the 1950s song Bingo, Bango, Bongo, I don't wanna leave the Congo or, They're rioting in Africa. You won't hear, "Hey, thanks. You're a real white man!" or "That's very white of you." Nor will your small children hear their teacher say, "Here are the little books I promised you: *The Story of Little Black Sambo* and Uncle Remus's *Brer Rabbit and The Tar Baby*!" or "Let's all put on our thinking caps and..." Or more to the point: "And as for you, Tyrone, (a black boy) you go over to the high stool in the corner and put on that dunce cap. Listen carefully and perhaps you'll begin to understand what the rest of us are talking about. But if you fall asleep again be careful you don't fall and hurt yourself," then turning back to the rest of the class and lowering her voice. "Some of them just can't get it."

Seventy percent of all NFL (National Football League) players are Afro-American. NFL leaders, now painfully aware of the dangers of CTE (Chronic Traumatic Encephalopathy), have begun awarding compensation to former players. However, the amount given to black players is less than that received by their white counterparts. As the reason for this, they, the NFL, claimed that blacks are less susceptible to the worst effects of CTE. In their own words, "blacks started with lower cognitive functions," and that this adjudication was based on what the NFL called "race norming." Are we edging back to the days of Charles Murray's highly controversial book, *The Bell Curve* (1994) which, co-authored with Richard J. Herrstein, concluded that Afro-Americans, as a race, measured fifteen points lower in IQ than whites? Furthermore, that in whites this difference was sixty percent "heritable," which indicates a genetic influence.

And why don't all those so-called Independents support a voting rights act, giving more Blacks the opportunity to vote? Yes, racism is the reason, but they won't admit it, though their actions, or should I say inaction in these days of "quiet" racism, proves it. Obama meant well, and he certainly has my respect, but despite his accomplishments (mainly health care) he merely made the white supremacists gnash their teeth all the harder (we should rename it the "Black House!"). One thing is clear, the harder the Democrats press for "progressive change", the more hardened the Republicans will be.

Anti-racism, or whatever euphemism is in vogue now, cannot be legislated any more than telling people what to eat, or whom to love, or any other personal choices that are not illegal. If people prefer to be in the company of certain people and not others, you cannot gainsay them.

Police brutality among blacks continues increasingly, and the consequences which would be appropriate to the perpetrators are swept under the rug of police immunity as soon as conveniently possible, aided by the state policies that help to do it. In Germany, to cite only one of many other developed nations, *all* police aspirants are required to successfully complete a training course of two years. In the U.S. among the larger (city) police forces the course is a mere twenty weeks, and less in some rural areas, in some cases much less. Here lies another example of conflict between states' rights and the central government.

Why are Republicans causing a log jam in Congress by supporting Trump's lies about those presidential election results? Why are the republican governors of fourteen states recounting the election results for the third time, and in the case of Arizona it might be the fourth, (I've lost count)? Are we developing into a nation wherein lies are as acceptable as the truth?

We don't know how many members of Congress actually believe Trump's lies and how many go along with him for their own selfish interests. I think the latter outnumber the former. Whatever the case, if Trump had anything like a decent education he might mutter contentedly: *Oderint dum metuant*—Let them hate provided they fear. And in keeping with their almost fanatical pursuit of partisanship, Republican Senators have made it clear that they intend to stall the 1/6 committee hearings by filibustering until the coming mid-term elections. A great part of the problem lies in the fact that the Executive Branch of the Federal government hasn't the power, at least during a time of crisis such as the one we are in, to mandate, not ask, the states to take such actions and not certain others for the benefit of the entire nation. Certainly our Judicial Branch hasn't been able to do it. And incidentally, if a Constitutional Convention were ever to be held, Article III should be revised to include the following: should there still be the two major parties in the Congress there will be four judges from each party seated on the Court. In the event of a tie in any decision, the Chief Justice, who must be a sworn and vetted Independent, will break it. We can only hope that our days of lying by governmental officials, both elected and appointed, will be alleviated by such a change.

Despite the platitudinous pronouncements made recently by Mitch McConnell, Senate Majority Leader and premier coward among the many others in the ranks of Republican members of Congress who meekly follow Trump's lying pronouncements in order to ensure their job security in their states and districts, our system of democracy is in total disarray. It is rapidly becoming its own worst enemy. Americans are too unruly, too ignorant,[*] and too indifferent to enjoy (and deserve) a truly democratic system of governance. Added to those disabilities, we have no cohesive, common philosophy, religion, no culture that isn't larded with sex, violence, drugs, and "body art" to be proud of; relatively little history to be boastful of, and a good deal more that has brought us dishonor—slavery, genocide of Native Americans, interference, often bloody, in the affairs of other sovereign nations, to name a few—all of which makes our highly-touted "great melting pot" boastfulness a bit of a fraud. We actually are falsely proud of those very qualities I listed which would not divide us but give us the cohesive strength we need to become a truly great nation. And too many of our people have been led to believe that our form of democracy has its inherent safeguards against the deadly issues that we now face. To deny assurances such as those made so blithely by Senator McConnell would be abhorrent to them.

So once again, what can we do to resolve the ills which we ourselves have brought upon this country? We must reform our system of governance; but how? We have looked

---

[*] Almost thirty percent of Americans are functionally illiterate—can't understand the instructions on a medicine bottle or a recipe in a cookbook—while ten percent are totally illiterate. Many of these get the "truth" on newscasts from their favorite TV news channels such as Fox News.

at other forms and found them lacking, even repugnant and dangerous. No totalitarian system is to be considered. But perhaps there is a milder authoritarian design worthy of consideration, not the kind exemplified by Trump in John Dean's recent book *Authoritarian Nightmare* (2021); not autocracy; certainly not socialism, at least not the type too many untutored Americans referred to as the "pinko" type that is only one step away from communism; not even the social democracy Bernie Sanders sometimes seems to suggest and that is practiced in several countries around the world.

In the latter part of the eighteenth century, the crowned heads of Europe, all absolute, unchallenged rulers, in consideration for their subjects somehow tacitly agreed to practice what historians refer to as Enlightened Despotism; a series of social, educational, legal, economic reforms springing from the Renaissance and driven by the profound crises of two great wars.* This period was brief historically, lasting only about twenty years. Now if we could reserve and respect that word "enlightened" and eschew that "despotism" with all its distasteful connotations, perhaps we could develop something useful for our search. It would be well to keep in mind what my namesake, Blaise Pascal, French philosopher and mathematician, wrote 400 years ago: "Justice without strength is helpless, strength without justice is tyrannical."

So to establish a new structure of government, at least *pro tempore*, and to reestablish our democracy, starting at the highest level of executive power, we must have a leader, a strong but just and compassionate president—I picture the

---

* The War of the Austrian Succession and The Seven Years' War.

model of the venerable actor Donald Crisp, the sometimes stern but kindhearted father he portrayed so well in several films (or, I hasten to add, his female counterpart). To find and nominate such a person would require a select "blue ribbon" committee to conduct the search for and vetting of such a candidate. I would suggest an Independent with the same qualifications as the proposed Chief Justice of the Supreme Court I described earlier, to avoid nominating a potential cat's paw of either of the two existing parties. Finally, the nominee would need approval by a two-thirds vote of both houses of Congress. A popular vote almost invariably would be fruitless since this "good father" (or mother)* might be an unknown professor of political science from somewhere in academia. He or she certainly would not be made prominent by a lengthy and expensive campaign with all its media coverage (about which more later). Once in office, this person would be surrounded and supported by a cabinet of experts in every field and discipline who would be provided by a similar process as that which I recommended for the President. Under a war powers act, this group, which would make up the Executive Branch of the central government, would have broader scope and be less affected by constitutional limitations than any other powers of government, especially of the general government in a federal system such as that of the United States.

Now what benefits would accrue to such a system, however temporary, to see us through this true emergency we have created? To begin with, a constitutional convention could and should be authorized by the new government

---

* It's difficult for a man of my age to satisfy "the dark divinities of feminism" (Dickens), but I *am* trying.

without approval or interference by the legislative or judicial branches of government or that of the states. Such a convention would serve to review, and where necessary, to revise portions of the entire document to include its amendments. The convention should be as brief as possible, consistent with the revisions deemed necessary (unlike most government processes which today move at a snail's pace). Both houses of Congress should not be made to reconvene until the convention was adjourned; then they would be made to implement the changes to the constitution without debate or delay.

These changes should include, but not be limited to: eliminating the electoral college; reapportioning senatorial representation according to state population—Montana, with less than a million people, has as much voting and other powers in the Senate as California, with forty million; all processes, protocols, and procedures involving needless or nonessential time should be strictly controlled to avoid the undue passage of time or delay; as in the case of George Floyd and his killer Officer Derek Chauvin.* Witness the more than two months between the last presidential election and Inauguration Day and the consequent harm done by Trump and his lackeys during the interim, to include that infamous insurrection of January 6th, petty criminals who can't afford bail are languishing in jail while awaiting trial (the right to a *speedy* and public trial under the Fourth Amendment?); prisoners awaiting execution are dying of old age before their execution day arrives or writing and

---

* In what should have been an "open and shut case," it took a year to try him and another month to sentence him. The killer was well named; viz. Chauvin, the excessive patriot and devotee of Napoleon (in a play), hence chauvinism, chauvinistic.

publishing one or more books while awaiting that fateful day; if we get back to campaigning for federal elective office, a drastic reduction should be mandated in the length of campaigns and the funds expended on them (to the benefit of the media outlets and others hosting candidates on the stump). Political campaigns in other developed nations last for a few weeks or less, while ours go on for almost three years, and our elected officials begin looking for contributions for the next election on the day they take office; states' rights versus federal necessity or expediency (where a major part of our problems lie); resolving the dilemma of that notorious Second Amendment, to which I have suggested what would be only a temporary solution earlier in this thesis—in any case, the original intent of that amendment (a well-ordered militia for each state to counter undue interference by the federal government) must be clarified once and for all if this horror of shootings is to be put to rest. Those are merely some of the revisions or clarifications needed in our sacred document no matter what the "originalists" try to tell you. But other matters than those of the constitution must be addressed also.

Reflecting upon what I have said about time lapses, it has been six months since the infamous January 6th attack on the Capitol building and the first culprit just came to stand before the Bar of Justice. In announcing some details of the hearing on the events of January 6th, 2021, Speaker of the House Nancy Pelosi, stated that the hearings would have "no time limit." They could do it in a week or two at the most. Under a new regime of jurisprudence, the people who have been identified as having participated in the Trump-inspired insurrection, and they number in the hundreds, should have been arrested, confined in a detention facility, and then sent to the U.S. prison at Guantanamo, Cuba to await further quick justice. While there, they should be kept on short rations, especially since so many of them are so morbidly obese. They all should be tried as domestic terrorists. And while on the subject of wasting time, let me suggest that the almost comic filibuster, a peculiarly American institution, should be done away with completely.

Still on the subject of the 6 January obscenity, it now has become clear that though intelligence sources had received credible indications that an attack was imminent, no adequate defenses were prepared. Further, that there was a significant space of time before forces adequate to quell the insurrectionists could respond. That our *seventeen* separate intelligence agencies were inadequate to the task, despite operating under the same central director and echoing the 9/11 disaster, makes reason totter on its rightful throne.

We should reduce the size of our armed forces drastically (except and unfortunately for our nuclear weapons and their delivery means as a safeguard against a hostile threat from Russia or now even North Korea). Our annual armed forces budget is almost a trillion dollars. If we want to begin saving money, that would be a good place to start. Why must we have twelve or thirteen aircraft carriers? China has one, and it is obsolete. Although the comparison is absurd, it does make a point; when Costa Rica disbanded its relatively small army many years ago its president announced: "Who would attack a country with no army?" In any case, if we did make a substantial reduction, we could save billions of dollars annually (some of it in bribes), by not having to maintain 700 military, air, and naval bases throughout the world and moving the personnel who man them on change of assignments, other official business, and leaves of absence.* And merely as a rather whimsical thought, we also might be inclined, in our foreign entanglements, to let other sovereign states settle their own problems and affairs, instead of interfering in the name of freedom and "democracy." Look at our record following WWII: we settled for a very shaky armistice after three years of bloody fighting in Korea; we failed to rid Cuba of Fidel Castro and his communists in 1961; the communists drove us humiliatingly out of Vietnam in 1975 after we had killed, needlessly and fruitlessly, two or three million innocent civilians; then after invading Iraq for no good reason (except perhaps just to exact revenge on *someone* after the 9/11 attack and to kill Saddam Hussein, and the only result is that we've left Iraq a perfect shambles; we've spent twenty years and over a trillion dollars in Afghanistan and accomplished nothing except to leave the Al Qaeda–ISIS-connected Taliban stronger than it was when we went in there, and now, when we're withdrawing our troops, shamelessly deserting thousands of loyal translators and interpreters and their families to a fate that can only be imagined and doesn't bear thinking about (and what about those 1,000 Afghan soldiers fleeing into Tajikistan?). Additionally, twenty-two Afghan special troops, trained by U.S. Special Forces, were killed as they tried to surrender to the Taliban. And what about Zalmay Yamani, the translator-interpreter who received political

---

* Of interest is the fact that Israel, "our greatest ally in the Middle East," except for the few Marines at our embassy there, will not permit us to establish a single military, air, or naval base on Israeli soil, or even share their own bases with us as the NATO countries do, despite the fact that we provide them with four to five billion dollars in foreign aid each year.

asylum in the U.S. and now is being deported back to Afghanistan because it was discovered that, when a child, he gave bread to a Taliban soldier! All this, and still we talk unblushingly about bringing democracy to the rest of the world, and especially now, when our own democratic system is showing all the signs of incipient failure. Incidentally, and though I don't credit this, there are revisionist historians who claim that if the Italians had had the will to fight on, if the Germans hadn't run out of oil and men, and it weren't for the "Russian (Soviet) Steam Roller" and the atom bomb, the eastern half of America would be speaking German and the western half Japanese. When will we learn that you can't make everyone sit down to a square meal?

Under the same war powers act, we could nationalize certain industries and utilities in keeping with the ammunition restriction I spoke of and to counter the current cyber threat to our infrastructure, and do it under a central control. Defense against these cyber attacks, while left to manufacturers of the equipment needed to counter them, will provide us with only a scattered system of safeguards and proper response and so lower their effectiveness. Sooner or later our power grid(s) will be attacked, and in this modern electronic age there is little that doesn't operate on electric power; even the best lithium-ion batteries don't last forever. Our children have become so dependent on electronic devices they don't even know how to hold a pen or a pencil properly, or solve simple arithmetical problems without a calculator. In other writing, I have described the horrors that would ensue if our power were to be cut off indefinitely. A few hours or even a day would be manageable; to have no idea when you'll have that all essential power again would result in panic followed by utter chaos. Think of what would be the state of hospitals during this long night. You may speak of generators, but like those batteries they can't provide power when their fuel runs out. To cite just one more effect, another that hardly bears thinking about, the suicide rate would skyrocket, and no amount of anti-depression pills would stop it from doing so.

However grim that last possibility, let's go on to something more tangible. As part of our infrastructure revitalization program, if Congress and the President can ever agree about funding, we should rebuild our railway system. We once had the best rail system in the world. Trains were everywhere, reaching every small town and even villages, where they would stop even if only to bring the mail and perhaps drop off or pick up a little cargo. We still have freight trains but not so many as would keep those increasingly large and too numerous tractor-trailers that go everywhere, both day and night, tearing up what's left of our highways. I haven't been to Germany for many years, but it seems that when I was there, restrictions were on those big trucks, such as only being able to use those wonderful *Autobahns* during the hours of midnight and 6A.M. and were prohibited from going through the smaller towns and villages altogether. General Eisenhower came back from Europe after the war with admiration of those German highways built by Hitler in the 1930s. So impressed was he that without delay, once he became President, he initiated a highway system we still are using. However, either we're not the road builders the Germans are, or we don't maintain them as well, or both. I think both are true, since our highways, as well as our bridges, tunnels, and our physical infrastructure in general are falling apart. At least two important changes were caused by Eisenhower's enthusiasm: our passenger railroad network virtually disappeared, and the automobile industry has been booming since those highways were built, providing untold impetus to our greatest threat and challenge—climate change, which is producing global warming and which ultimately will kill every living thing on this planet. So why should we go and explore Mars at great expense when we can achieve the same desolation right here on Mother Earth? Or rather, should we build some passenger-carrying bullet trains and get rid of a hundred million gas burning cars?

We must establish an immigration system worthy of the name. Perhaps when we've satisfied our requirements for lettuce and fruit pickers in California's "salad bowl" and elsewhere, we should follow the example of countries such as New Zealand and Switzerland, who require that immigrants have some professional qualification or prove that they have a certain amount of money, or both, before they can apply for citizenship. There certainly should be a requirement to learn just enough of the English language to understand it and be understood, since most Americans don't speak anything except English, and even that not very well.

To reestablish a true middle class, we must address the inequitable distribution of wealth in this potentially rich and great nation. Mainly, the only people who can invest seriously in stocks and bonds don't need the profits they receive and can afford to lose money if they do. The people on "Main Street" barely have enough money to go on with. During the pandemic many lost their jobs and won't get them back, while those still employed can't afford even as little as $400 in the event of a family emergency. And who can afford to retire more or less comfortably anymore? Many honest people are literally working themselves into the grave. While the pandemic was raging and seemingly uncontrollable, the stock market was booming. And do you think the pharmaceutical houses that are supplying those vaccines are doing it for free? With one percent of the people in this country controlling ninety percent of its wealth, we *must* raise taxes on the banks and large corporations, many of which, through the "creative" bookkeeping of their accountants and lawyers and their "K" Street lobbyists in Washington, continue to pay no taxes at all (!). I could go on with this, but if I do, I'll be writing another book. In any case, the list of ills remains virtually endless.

As I said earlier, most Americans don't know what true democracy is, to say nothing about its real benefits if the system of governance is conducted properly, justly, and honestly. Of course, those three qualities won't be worth a tinker's curse, nor will all the benefits if (when) global warming has its way. So in consonance with all the changes I've suggested and as a vital beginning, why don't we stop digging our own graves

To end this screed, I'd like to say something about President Biden and what he presently is confronted with. First and of most immediate concern is the passing of a voting rights act which (somehow) mandates the rules all states must follow in their elections for federal office holders. If proper rules are not laid down *and enforced*, given the number of Trump-supporting governors and the margin of his loss in the last election, Trump may well be elected President in 2024. Biden must take some action or find other means to ensure that such a catastrophe, for that is what it would be; the last knell of our democracy, is avoided. So, what to do? There still is enough time to reorganize or at least to rearrange our policy so as to give the Executive Branch of our central government more power. This objective could begin with invoking a war powers act, as I have described. I have suggested a systemic change to follow, but that is only one solution; more thought and study by the president's top advisors may reveal another and better approach.

One thing is clear: at least for the present those palmier and more sensible days Biden may recall during his time as a Senator, when crossing the aisle to confer with a Republican colleague on compromise was a common practice, and as in diplomacy was essential to moulding adequate and mutually agreeable legislation. But those days are over, at least for the foreseeable future. There is much more that our well-intentioned but much beleaguered president must contend with, but as a good commander must go where the enemy threat is greatest, Biden must set his actions in priority order. It will take everything he has left, both moral and physical, to succeed; if he somehow manages to do so he will find his place in the history books as one of our greatest leaders, so daunting is the task before him. Still, at the risk of being somewhat facetious, I see him as a man valiantly trying to shoot pool with a hockey stick.

As to what I've said about the threat of Trump's possible victory in 2024, there is this. Apropos of holding a Constitutional Convention for the purpose of revision and clarification in order to suit today's needs we could avoid the calamity of a loose cannon such as Donald J.

Trump from holding any political office again. This would be accomplished by broadening the provisions of the 25th Amendment to include mental instability as the reason a president is unable to discharge the powers and duties of his office. Trump has been diagnosed as having been a paranoid narcissist since early adulthood.[*] Would it not be, as a sensible precaution after having suffered the enduring damage wrought by putting a mad man in the White House for four years, to require a psychological screening of both candidates who win the primary presidential elections? If the Constitution were revised, would it not be wise to include such a requirement in Article II?

When I listened to the news this morning I heard: The Great Salt Lake in Utah has almost dried up; uncontrolled fires are raging in the Far West; hundreds of Europeans are drowning in the floods there; COVID-19 cases and consequent deaths are rising everywhere at an alarming rate due to the "Delta" variant of the disease and the refusal to get vaccinated by those who—if you'll permit me a sad little pun—could be known as true die-hards; and inflation is setting in steadily. Ah well, "If it bleeds, it leads," as the old journalistic injunction dictates.

And with that I'll bid you an affectionate farewell and wish you a not-too-dismal future. *Ebbene, la commedia è finita.*

---

[*] On February 13th 2017 a group of thirty-five psychiatrists, psychologists, and social workers published a letter in *The New York Times* stating that "Mr. Trump's speech and actions make him incapable of serving as president…a form of narcissism so extreme that it affects a person's ability to perform…need for admirations, and lack of empathy, beginning by early boyhood and present in a variety of contexts."